A COLLECTION OF PERFORMANCE TASKS AND RUBRICS:

HIGH SCHOOL MATHEMATICS

Charlotte Danielson
and Elizabeth Marquez

EYE ON EDUCATION
6 DEPOT WAY WEST, SUITE 106
LARCHMONT, NY 10538
(914) 833-0551 phone
(914) 833-0761 fax

Library of Congress Cataloging-in-Publication Data

Danielson, Charlotte.
  A collection of performance tasks and rubrics : high school
mathematics / by Charlotte Danielson and Elizabeth Marquez.
      p.   cm.
  ISBN 1-883001-49-8
  1. Mathematics - - Study and teaching (Secondary) - -
Evaluation.
  I. Marquez, Elizabeth. II. Title.
QA11.D3453 1998
510'.71'2 - - dc21   97-38988
                                                              CIP

 PRINTED IN CANADA

Published by Eye On Education:

A Collection of Performance Tasks and Rubrics:
Upper Elementary Mathematics
by Charlotte Danielson

A Collection of Performance Tasks and Rubrics:
Middle School Mathematics
by Charlotte Danielson

The Performance Assessment Handbook
Volume 1 Portfolios and Socratic Seminars
by Bil Johnson

The Performance Assessment Handbook
Volume 2 Performances and Exhibitions
by Bil Johnson

Performance Assessment and Standards-Based Curriculum
by Allan Glatthorn with Don Bragaw, Karen Dawkins,
and John Parker

Teaching in the Block
by Robert Lynn Canady and Michael D. Rettig

Instruction and the Learning Environment
by James Keefe and John Jenkins

The Reflective Supervisor: A Practical Guide for Educators
by Ray Calabrese and Sally Zepeda

Action Research on Block Scheduling
by David Marshak

Block Scheduling: A Catalyst for Change in High Schools
by Robert Lynn Canady and Michael D. Rettig

Bringing the NCTM Standards to Life: Best Practices from
Elementary Educators
by Lisa Owen and Charles Lamb

Mathematics the Write Way: Activities for
Every Elementary Classroom
by Marilyn Neil

Research on Educational Innovations
by Arthur Ellis and Jeffrey Fouts

Research on School Restructuring
by Arthur Ellis and Jeffrey Fouts

**The School Porfolio: A Comprehensive Framework
for School Improvement**
by Victoria Bernhardt

Educator's Brief Guide to Computers in the Schools
by Eugene F. Provenzo Jr.

Educator's Brief Guide to the Internet and the Worldwide Web
by Eugene F. Provenzo Jr.

Handbook of Educational Terms and Applications
by Arthur Ellis and Jeffrey Fouts

Leadership: A Relevant and Realistic Role for Principals
by Gary Crow, L. Joseph Matthews, and Lloyd McCleary

Leadership through Collaboration: Alternatives to the Hierarchy
by Michael Koehler and Jeanne Baxter

The Principal as Steward
by Jack McCall

The Principal's Edge
by Jack McCall

Hands-On Leadership Tools for Principals
by Ray Calabrese, Gary Short, and Sally Zepeda

School-to-Work
by Arnold Packer and Marion Pines

Schools for all Learners: Beyond the Bell Curve
by Renfro Manning

ABOUT THE AUTHORS

Charlotte Danielson is president of Princeton Education Associates in Princeton, New Jersey and Senior Associate for Assessment for the Council for Basic Education in Washington, DC. She has worked as a consultant on performance assessment for numerous schools and school districts in the United States and overseas. Recent publications include *Enhancing Professional Practice: A Framework for Teaching*, and *Teaching for Understanding*, both published by ASCD.

Elizabeth Marquez, winner of the Presidential Award for Excellence in Mathematics Teaching, teaches mathematics at North Brunswick Township High School in New Jersey. She is a co-author of the New Jersey Standards for Teaching Mathematics, co-author of the *Prentice-Hall Mathematics Standardized Test Prep* and is a consultant to the Educational Testing Service.

ACKNOWLEDGMENTS

The authors would like to thank Fran Arbaugh, Rosemary Fogarty, Frank Lester, Jay McTighe, and Barry Shealy for offering comments on this book when it was in the manuscript stage.

The tasks "Get a Job" and "Mean Salary" were released from the New Jersey State Department of Education.

TABLE OF CONTENTS

FOREWORD

The *Curriculum and Evaluation Standards for School Mathematics* released by the National Council of Teachers of Mathematics (NCTM) have profoundly influenced the vision and practice of mathematics education. Through their call for a greater emphasis on problem solving, reasoning, and communications, the *Standards* have validated the expanded use of performance tasks for classroom instruction and assessment. Effective performance tasks call for such reasoning and communication by engaging students in applying mathematical concepts and skills in the context of "authentic" problems.

While educators generally understand and support the recommendations of NCTM to incorporate performance tasks for assessment purposes, a number of practical questions remain – how do teachers develop "authentic" tasks to assess students' understanding, reasoning and mathematical communication?; how does the use of performance tasks fit with more traditional forms of assessment in mathematics?; how do teachers evaluate student responses since performance tasks typically call for more than a single, correct answer?

Charlotte Danielson and Elizabeth Marquez offer timely and practical answers in this readable guide to the development and use of performance tasks and rubrics in high school classrooms. The book provides an excellent overview of the rationale for, and the strengths and limitations of, the use of performance tasks to assess student achievement and progress in mathematics. They offer a user-friendly, field-tested process for developing performance tasks and rubrics, along with practical advice for evaluating student work, selecting "anchors", and establishing performance standards. Finally, the sample tasks, rubrics and student work samples provide "tried and true" resources for immediate use, while serving as models to guide development of additional tasks and scoring tools.

Readers of *A Collection of Performance Tasks and Rubrics* will not be confronted with an "ivory tower" treatise on what should be. Rather, they will discover a valuable resource, grounded in the wisdom of years of experience in schools and classrooms, for making the NCTM vision come to life.

— Jay McTighe
Director, Maryland Assessment Consortium

PREFACE

Educators have recognized for some time the unique role of assessment in the classroom environment. Assessment provides valuable information for both teachers and students regarding how well everyone is doing. Students can see where they went wrong in their understanding; and teachers can determine whether a concept needs to be re-taught. This function, of monitoring progress on valued learning goals, is the first purpose of assessment, and one that supports every other purpose.

Assessment also defines what students must know and be able to do to succeed in a particular teacher's class; students frequently say that they don't know, until they have seen a teacher's first tests in the fall, just what that person values. Is this person a stickler for details? Or are the big ideas all that is important? When teachers coach their students in how to prepare for a test, they are conveying what is important, both to them and in the subject. Such coaching can serve a clarifying purpose for teachers as well as students; by specifying what their students should study in preparation for a test, and in designing that test, teachers must confront their subject and make decisions about what is truly important.

However, there is much more to assessment than simply monitoring of student progress and clarifying expectations. Because most tests "count," they motivate as well. That is, to the extent that tests or other assessments are used to calculate students' grades, students will try to do well. Tests can "count" for teachers as well. In some towns, for example, scores on standardized tests are published in the newspaper; student scores on AP tests are seen as reflections on their teachers' instructional skills; and some states and school districts use test scores as the basis for rewards or sanctions. When test scores matter, teachers will attempt to have their students do well. And while few teachers will engage in unethical practices, most teachers will provide instruction in such a manner as to assist their students in performing as well as they can.

But it is not only in defining the content that tests and other assessments influence practice. The form matters as well. That is, when students are asked on tests (and know in advance that they will be asked) to answer a number of multiple-choice or short-answer questions, they tend to prepare in that manner, committing to memory that which they predict will be on the test. If deeper understanding is not required for the test, they may not strive to achieve it. If a question is ambiguous, they will seek to "read the mind" of the teacher, to determine the right answer even if they believe another is better.

The form of assessments also affects teachers' practices. If a test does not require, or does not reward, understanding, why should teachers emphasize it in their own classrooms? If all that is needed in mathematics, for example, is for students to get the right answer (possibly without understanding why the procedure works) then the procedure is all that will be provided in some classrooms.

Assessments matter, therefore, both in what they assess and how they assess it. The content of a test affects what students study and teachers teach, and the form of the assessment affects how they approach the task. Teachers have discovered, for example, that if they want their students to become better writers, they must make good writing count in the classroom; they must teach it systematically and assess it authentically. A test of correcting errors, for example, will not do; they must assess students' actual writing. Similarly, if teachers want students to acquire skills in solving mathematical problems, or communicating their mathematical ideas, they must both teach and assess those skills.

These considerations have provided much of the energy behind the movement towards "performance assessment," that is, students actually creating or constructing an answer to a question. Teachers and policy-makers alike have discovered that when assessment tasks more accurately mirror the types of learning goals they have for students -- both in the content and the form of assessment -- the learning environment is transformed. The assessments themselves tend to be motivational and engaging; students invest energy in the tasks and commit to them. In addition, performance assessments even serve to educate as well as assess student learning; teachers find that their students learn from doing performance tasks.

However, performance assessment has one enormous drawback; it is time-consuming to do, both to design and to work into classroom instructional time. Even teachers who are committed to the practice of performance assessment find that they don't have time to design good performance tasks, to try them out with students, and perfect them for later use. Furthermore, most teachers did not learn to design performance tasks and scoring rubrics as part of their professional preparation. And while many educators have learned such skills as part of their continuing professional growth, they may lack the confidence to use such performance tasks as a central part of their assessment plan.

This book is designed to address this need. It is based on the assumption that many educators are interested in incorporating performance assessment into their classroom routines, but have either not yet acquired the technical skill or do not have the time required to design them on their own. This book provides a collection of performance tasks and scoring rubrics for a number of topics in upper elementary school mathematics, which teachers can use as is, or adapt for their students and their particular situation. It is intended to save time for busy educators, to provide examples of tested performance tasks. The samples of student work provide a range of responses, to clarify the tasks, and to anchor the points on the scoring rubrics.

Chapter One provides the reader with an introduction to performance assessment and how it is distinguished from traditional testing. Chapter Two offers a rationale for performance assessment, explaining its strengths (and its drawbacks) as compared with more traditional approaches. In Chapter Three the reader can find guidance in making an evaluation plan, and linking that plan to the overall approach to curriculum development. Chapter Four consists of an overview of evaluating complex performance, and includes a description of evaluating non-school (and yet complex) performance that can be used in a workshop setting to introduce educators to performance assessment. Chapters Five and Six offer a step-by-step procedure for creating a performance task and a rubric for classroom use, while Chapter Seven suggests techniques for adapting an existing performance task for use in one's own classroom. Chapter Eight is the heart of the collection, and offers performance tasks (some with samples of student work) and rubrics, covering the major topics in high school mathematics, designed to be adapted, or used as is, in your classroom. The Appendix contains handouts of each of the 21 tasks which may be photocopied and distributed to students.

1

INTRODUCTION

This book concerns the classroom use of performance assessment, and the evaluation of student work in response to performance tasks. It contains a collection of performance tasks in high school mathematics, but also includes guidance for educators to design or adapt performance tasks for their own use.

While performance assessment is essential to a well-rounded assessment plan, it should not be used exclusively. Traditional testing has an important role to play, particularly in assessing a large domain or evaluating student knowledge. But in assessing student understanding, in order to ascertain how well students can apply their knowledge, some type of performance assessment is essential.

In this book, performance assessment means any assessment of student learning that requires the evaluation of student writing, products, or behavior. That is, it includes all assessment with the exception of multiple choice, matching, true/false testing, or problems with a single correct answer. Classroom-based performance assessment includes all such assessment that occurs in the classroom and is evaluated by teachers as distinct from large-scale, state-wide performance testing programs.

Performance assessment is fundamentally criterion-referenced rather than norm-referenced. That is, teachers who adopt performance assessment are concerned with the degree to which students can demonstrate knowledge and skill in a certain field. They know what it means to demonstrate competence; the purpose of a performance assessment is to allow students to show what they can do. The criteria for evaluating performance are important; teachers use their professional judgment in establishing such criteria and defining levels of performance. And the standards they set for student performance are typically above that expected for minimal competency; they define accomplished performance.

Norm-referenced tests are less valuable to teachers than are performance assessments. True, teachers may learn what their students can do compared to other students of the same age. However, the items on the test may or may not reflect the curriculum of a given school or district; to the extent that these are different, the information provided may not be of value to the teacher. Moreover, the results of most standardized tests are not known for some time. Even for those items included in a school's curriculum, it does not help a teacher to know in June, that a student did not know, in April, a concept that was taught the previous November. Of what possible use is that information to the teacher in June? It may not even still be true. And even if true, the information comes too late to be useful.

In addition, the only way students demonstrate progress on a norm-referenced test is in comparison to other students. Progress *per se* is not shown as progress. That is, a student's standing may move from the 48th percentile to the 53rd percentile. However, the student may not have learned much but other students may have learned less! So while norm-referenced tests have their value, for example for large-scale program evaluation, they are of limited use to teachers who want to know what their students have learned. Performance assessment, then, is criterion-referenced. It reflects the curriculum goals of a teacher, school, or district, and when used in the context of classroom teaching, it informs instructional decisions. In the remaining sections of this chapter, the different uses and types of performance assessment are described.

SUMMARY

Classroom based performance assessment is criterion-referenced and is used to evaluate student learning on clearly identified instructional goals. As such, it should be designed to be of optimal usefulness to its different audiences: teachers, students, and parents.

THE USES OF CLASSROOM-BASED PERFORMANCE ASSESSMENT

Assessment of student learning in the classroom is done for many purposes and can serve many ends. When teachers design their assessment strategies, it is helpful to determine, at the outset, which of the many possible uses they have in mind. Some possibilities are described here.

INSTRUCTIONAL DECISION-MAKING

Many teachers discover, after they have taught a concept, that many students didn't "get it;" that, while they may have had looks of understanding on their faces, and may have participated in the instructional activities, they are unable to demonstrate the knowledge or understanding on their own.

This is important information for teachers to have, as they determine what to do next with a class, or even with a few students. They may decide that they must re-teach the concept, or create a different type of instructional activity. Alternatively, if only a few students lack understanding, a teacher might decide to work with them separately, or to design an activity which can be used for peer tutoring.

Whatever course of action a teacher decides upon, however, it is decided on the basis of information regarding student understanding. That implies that the assessment strategies used will reveal student understanding, or lack of it. And when used for instructional decision-making, it is the teacher alone who uses the information. The results of the assessment are not shared with students, nor are they used for grading. The assessment is solely for the teacher's benefit, to determine whether the instructional activities achieved their intended purpose.

FEEDBACK TO STUDENTS

Performance assessment, like any assessment, may also be used to provide feedback to students regarding their progress. Depending on how it is constructed, a performance task can let students know in which dimensions of performance they excel, and in which they need to devote additional energy. Such feedback is, by its nature, individualized; the feedback provided to one student will be very different from that provided to another if their performances are different. It is efficient for the teacher, however, since the important dimensions of performance have been identified beforehand.

COMMUNICATION WITH PARENTS

Actual student performance on well-designed tasks can provide parents with authentic evidence of their child's level of functioning. Many parents are skeptical of tests which they don't understand, and are not sure of the meaning of numbers, percentiles and scalene scores. But student answers to an open-ended question are easy to understand and can serve to demonstrate to parents the level of performance of their child. These samples of student work are highly beneficial for open house or parent conferences, to validate the judgments of the teacher.

Such indication of student performance is of particular importance if a teacher is concerned about a child and wants to persuade a parent that action is needed. It is impossible for parents, when confronted with the work of their own child, to question the commitment of the teacher in meeting that child's needs. Whether the work is exemplary and the teacher is recommending a more advanced placement, or the work reveals poor understanding, the actual samples of student performance are invaluable to a teacher in making a case for action.

SUMMATIVE EVALUATION OF STUDENT LEARNING

Like any assessment strategy, a performance assessment may be used to evaluate student learning and may contribute to decisions regarding grades. The issue of grading is complex and will be addressed more fully on page 19 of this book, but the results from performance tasks, like any assessment, can serve to substantiate a teacher's judgment in assigning a grade.

SUMMARY

Classroom-based assessment may be used for several different purposes. An overall assessment plan will take all desired purposes into account.

DIFFERENT TYPES OF CLASSROOM-BASED ASSESSMENT

Assessment takes many forms, depending on the types of instructional goals being assessed, and the use to which the assessment will be put. The major types are presented in table form, and are described below.

TESTS

Tests are listed as the first major column in Figure 1.1. They have always been (and will continue to be) an important method for ascertaining what students know and can do. When teachers decide to move to more authentic aspects of performance in order to evaluate student learning, they do not abandon tests. On the contrary, they use tests for those types of assessment for which they are well suited (for example, for sampling knowledge), recognizing their substantial strengths as a methodology.

Tests are generally given to students under what we call "testing conditions," that is, conditions that ensure that we are actually getting the authentic work of individuals and that the experience is the same for all students. Testing conditions are:

- *Limited time.* Generally speaking, time for a test is strictly limited. Students must complete the test within a certain amount of time (frequently a class period, but sometimes

FIGURE 1.1 FORMS OF ASSESSMENT

TEST		PRODUCT		BEHAVIOR	
Multiple-Choice	Constructed Response	Written	Physical	Structured	Spontaneous

Adapted from a worksheet developed by the Maryland Assessment Consortium.

more or less than that.) This provision ensures that some students don't devote far greater time to the assignments than others.

- *Limited (or no) resources.* Although there are exceptions to this rule (such as open-book tests), students taking a test are usually not permitted to consult materials as they work. An insistence on no additional resources rules out, of course, trips to the library while taking a test. This provision ensures that what students produce on the test reflects only their own understanding.

- *No talking with peers or looking on others' papers.* When taking a test, it is important that students produce their own work. Unless teachers adhere to this condition, they are never sure whether what they receive from an individual student reflects that student's understanding, or that of his or her friends.

In addition, tests are of two basic types: Select and Constructed-response.

- *Multiple choice.* In a multiple-choice test, students select the best answer from those given. True/false and matching tests may also be included in this category. Short-answer items are technically constructed response items (since the student supplies the answer), but since there is generally a single right answer, such items are a special case, and share more characteristics in their scoring with multiple-choice items.

- *Constructed-response.* In a constructed-response test, students answer a question in their own words. Open-ended questions are constructed response, as are essay questions on a test.

Of course, a single test may contain a combination of multiple-choice and constructed-response items. In fact, most tests do; they generally consist of some multiple-choice, true/false, short-answer, or matching items for a portion of the test and several essays for the remainder. The balance between these different types of test items varies enormously, by subject, grade level, and the preference of the teacher.

PRODUCT

A product is any item produced by students which is evaluated according to established criteria. A product is a thing, a physical object, and is generally (but not always) produced by students outside of school time. Students may take as long as they want and need to, and may consult books and speak with other people. Products may be one of two types: written or physical.

- *Written products.* A written product may be a term paper, an essay for homework, a journal entry, a drama, or a lab report. It is anything written by students, but not under testing conditions.

- *Physical products.* A physical product may be, for example, a diorama, a science construction, a project in industrial arts, or a sculpture. Physical products are three-dimensional things, and take up space.

Some projects done by students represent a combination of written and physical products. For example, most science fair projects consist of a physical construction of some sort, combined with a written description of the scientific principles involved.

Products are a rich source of information for teachers in seeking to understand what their students know and can do. However, they have a significant disadvantage, which limits their usefulness for high-stakes assessment. This relates to authenticity. When a student turns in a project, the teacher has no way of knowing the degree to which the work reflects the student's own knowledge and understanding, and the degree to which the student's parents or older siblings might have assisted.

For instructional purposes, most teachers encourage their students to obtain as much help as they can get; students are bound to learn more from an assignment with the insights of additional people. However, for purposes of assessment we need to know what each student can do; this requirement limits the usefulness of out-of-class assignments for evaluation. When used, they should be supplemented by other sources of information (for example, an assignment given under testing conditions) of which the teacher can be sure of authorship.

BEHAVIOR

Lastly, students demonstrate their knowledge or skill through their behavior, and this behavior can be evaluated. Behavior is that aspect of student performance which does not result in a tangible object; once completed, it is finished. However, behavior may be captured and stored, and then evaluated. For example, a skit may be videotaped, or a student reading aloud may be audiotaped. There are two types of behavior which may be used for evaluation:

- *Structured behavior.* In structured behavior, students are performing according to a pre-established framework. They may be staging a debate or a panel discussion. They may be giving a skit, performing a dance, or making a presentation. Teachers may be interviewing their students. Drama and speech classes depend on this type of performance to evaluate learning; it is useful in other fields as well. In virtually every state, acquiring a driver's license depends on successful performance behind the wheel.

- *Spontaneous behavior.* Students can also reveal their understanding through their spontaneous behavior. For example, their interaction when working on group projects, their questions during a discussion and their choices during free time, all demonstrate important aspects of their learning.

Because of the unstructured nature of spontaneous behavior, it is useful primarily as a supplemental form of assessment. However, for certain types of instructional goals, such as skill in collaboration, it may be the only appropriate form. The documentation of spontaneous behavior depends on careful observation. Many teachers use checklists so they can make their "kid watching" as systematic as possible.

SUMMARY

There are different types of classroom assessment. The major types include tests, products, and behavior. Depending on the types of instructional goals to be assessed, they are all valuable. For the purposes of this book all assessment except multiple-choice tests are considered performance assessment.

2

WHY PERFORMANCE ASSESSMENT?

It is clear that the design and implementation of performance assessment are far more time-consuming than the use of traditional tests. Why, one might ask, should a busy educator go to the trouble of changing? A good question, and one that deserves a thoughtful answer.

First, it should be made clear that when teachers use performance assessment, they don't stop using traditional forms of assessment. Tests will always be with us, and they should be. It is frequently important to ascertain what students know about a subject; alternatively, we must be sure that they have read an assignment. There is no substitute for a quiz or a test to ascertain these things. But as a steady diet, tests have serious limitations. These are described below.

THE LIMITATIONS OF TRADITIONAL TESTING

When we refer to "traditional testing" in this book, we mean multiple-choice, true/false, matching, or short-answer tests that teachers create or adapt for use in their classrooms. These are generally provided by the publishers of text programs, or have evolved over time. As noted above, they are useful for certain purposes (and they are certainly efficient to score), but when used exclusively, they have a negative influence.

VALIDITY

The most serious criticism of traditional tests is that the

range of student knowledge and skill that can be tested is extremely limited. Many aspects of understanding to which teachers and their communities are most committed simply don't lend themselves to multiple-choice assessment. To illustrate this point, it is helpful to identify the different categories of educational purposes (instructional goals) and to consider how they can be assessed.

There are, of course, many different ways to classify goals for this type of analysis; one comprehensive classification scheme is outlined below

- *Knowledge.* Most types of knowledge, whether procedural knowledge (i.e., how to wash lab equipment), conceptual understanding (i.e., the meaning of buoyancy), and the application of knowledge (i.e., determining the amount of paint needed to paint a room), may all be assessed through traditional means. Indeed, it is in the assessment of knowledge that traditional assessment rightfully exerts its strongest influence.

  Conceptual understanding, however, is not ideally suited to traditional testing since students can memorize, for example, a definition of "buoyancy" without really understanding it; their lack of understanding might not be revealed through a multiple-choice or matching test. It is only through their explanation of the concept in their own words, or their use of the concept in a problem that their understanding, or lack of it, is demonstrated.

- *Reasoning.* Traditional testing is poorly suited to the assessment of reasoning. While it is true that well-designed multiple-choice tests may be used to evaluate pure logic, most teachers without technical skills in this area are not advised to attempt it. Most of the reasoning we care about in schools (i.e., analyzing data, formulating and testing hypotheses, recognizing patterns) is better assessed through alternative means.

- *Communication.* In order to know whether students can

communicate, we must ask them to do so in writing or speaking. Attempts are made, of course, to evaluate students' understanding of written text and spoken language through multiple-choice tests. To some extent these attempts are successful but they rarely give teachers information they did not already have through more informal means. For the productive aspects of communication — writing and speaking — there is no substitute for students actually writing and speaking, and then evaluating their performance.

- *Skills.* Social skills and psychomotor skills are completely unsuited to traditional forms of assessment. A multiple-choice test on the rules of basketball does not tell a teacher whether or not a student can dribble the ball. And a matching test on how to work in groups does not convey whether students have actually acquired skills in collaboration. Nothing short of observation will do, using a carefully prepared observation guide. To the extent that skills are important aspects of learning, teachers must employ non-traditional assessment methods.

- *Affective Areas.* As with skills, traditional testing is entirely unsuited to the assessment of the affective domain. To the extent that teachers attempt to cultivate students' productive dispositions towards work (e.g., an open mind, pride in a job well done) they must look for little indicators through student behavior. As teachers try to cultivate an aesthetic sense in their students, for example appreciation of the mood of a poem, or the patterns in the multiplication tables, they must look for little comments and signs from their students. Other aspects of the affective domain are equally ill-matched to traditional testing, from self-confidence, to traits such as honesty and respect for private property, through the ability to weigh ethical arguments.

As is evident from the descriptions above, if teachers use only traditional forms of assessment, they will be unable to assess many aspects (some would say the most important aspects) of student learning. Clearly, other methods such as constructed-response tests, projects, and behavior are needed. These alternative modes must therefore be designed and procedures developed for the evaluation of student work produced through these alternative means.

DESIGN ISSUES

Measurement experts argue that most aspects of student knowledge and skill may be assessed through well-designed multiple-choice tests. They point to well-known tests that evaluate problem-solving, reasoning, and data analysis. On further examination, by looking at the actual items, most teachers would probably agree that the items require some higher-level thinking on the part of students.

Teachers should not assume because such test items are possible to construct that they themselves can construct them, or should want to spend the necessary time to do so. These test items are designed by measurement experts and are extensively field-tested to ensure that they are both valid and reliable. Neither of these conditions is available to most practicing educators, who have their next day's lessons to think about.

When teachers try to design their own multiple-choice tests, they encounter three related, though somewhat distinct, difficulties:

- *Ambiguity.* A major challenge confronting test developers is to create multiple-choice test items in which the wrong answers are plausible and yet, are unambiguously wrong. Ideally, the distracters (the wrong answers) should be incorrect in ways in which students' thinking is typically flawed, so a student's pattern of wrong answers may reveal diagnostic information.

  Such tests are very difficult to construct. Most teachers have had the experience of creating a test in which students can, by guessing or using a process of elimination, determine the right answer even when they know very little about the subject.

- *Authenticity.* In order to engage students in meaningful work, it is helpful for assessment to be as authentic as possible. Students are more likely to produce work of good quality if the questions seem plausible and worthwhile. But to design an authentic multiple-choice test, one that elicits the desired knowledge and skill, is very difficult. Highly authentic questions tend to be long and cumbersome, while more focused questions are often found to be boring and inauthentic by students.

- *Time.* Good multiple-choice questions require a great deal of time to create. And unless they are tested before being used, teachers cannot be sure that they are valid. That is, the question may be ambiguous, or several of the choices may be plausible. Hence, students are justified in challenging such questions and the evaluations based on them.

These factors, taken together, suggest that teachers are unlikely to be successful in creating their own multiple-choice tests for complex learning. Experts in test design can succeed more often than novices, but even experts are limited in what is possible through the technique.

INFLUENCE ON INSTRUCTION

Probably the most serious concern about the exclusive use of traditional testing relates to its effect on the instructional process. Since traditional tests are best suited to the assessment of low-level knowledge, such instructional goals are heavily represented (to the virtual exclusion of other, more complex, learning goals) in such tests.

It is well known that "what you test is what you get." Through our assessment methods we convey to students what is important to learn. And when the tests we give reflect only factual or procedural knowledge, we signal to students that such knowledge is more important than their ability to reason, to solve problems, to work together collaboratively, or to write effectively. Since multiple-choice tests are best at evaluating students' command of factual knowledge, many students equate school learning with trivial pursuit, and never realize that their teachers value the expression of their own ideas, a creative approach to problems, or the design of an imaginative experiment.

The most powerful means teachers have at their disposal for shifting the culture of their classrooms to one of significant work is to change their assessment methodologies. While traditional tests will always have a value, combining their use with alternative means sends an important signal to students regarding what sort of learning is valued in school. If good ideas and imaginative projects count, students will begin to shift their conceptions of the meaning of school.

SUMMARY

Traditional forms of assessment carry many disadvantages, which, when such tests are used exclusively, undermine the best intentions of teachers. These tests can evaluate only a narrow band of student learning and, even within that band, are extremely difficult to construct well.

THE BENEFITS OF PERFORMANCE ASSESSMENT

Many of the advantages of performance assessment are simply the reverse side of the limitations of traditional testing, namely, that they enable teachers to assess students in all those aspects of learning they value, in particular, writing and speaking, reasoning and problem solving, psychomotor and social skills, and the entire affective domain. However, there are many other benefits to be derived as well. These are described below.

CLARITY AS TO CRITERIA AND STANDARDS

When teachers use performance assessment, they discover that they must be extremely clear, both to themselves and to their students, as to the criteria they will use to evaluate student work, and the standard of performance they expect. For many teachers, this clarity is greater than that required for traditional testing, and requires that they give sustained thought to difficult questions such as "What do I really want my students to be able to do?" and "What is most important in this unit?" and "How good is good enough?"

These questions, while some of the most important that teachers ever consider, tend to be obscured by the pressure of daily work, and the normal routines of life in schools. The design of performance assessment tasks puts them at the center. Most teachers find that, while the questions are difficult to answer, their entire instructional program is greatly strengthened as a result of the effort.

PROFESSIONAL DIALOGUE ABOUT CRITERIA AND STANDARDS

If teachers create their performance assessments together, they must decide together how they will evaluate student work and what their standards will be. These are not easy discussions, but most teachers find them to be extremely valuable.

Occasionally, teachers find that their criteria for problem solving, for example, are very different from one another. One teacher may believe that the process used is more important than whether or not the answer is correct. Another may believe the reverse. They must resolve their differences in designing a problem-solving task, if they are to evaluate student work together. On the other hand, they could agree to disagree, and each use his or her own procedure. But the conversation will have been valuable in isolating such a fundamental difference in approach.

IMPROVED STUDENT WORK

Virtually all teachers report improved quality of student work when they begin using performance assessment. This is due, no doubt, to several factors:

- *Clarity as to criteria and standards.* Just as greater clarity as to criteria and standards is valuable to teachers and contributes to professional dialogue, it is essential for students. When students know what is expected, they are far more likely to be able to produce it than if they do not.

- *Greater confidence in work.* When students understand the criteria and standards to be used in evaluating their work, they can approach it with greater confidence. The criteria provide them with guidelines for their work and they can estimate the time required to produce work of good quality. All this tends to increase student engagement and pride in their work.

- *High expectations.* When they make the standards for exemplary performance clear to students, teachers are sending an important signal about their expectations. They are saying to students, in effect, "Here is how I define excellence. Anyone here can produce work of such quality by applying sufficient effort." This is a powerful message for students; it brings excellence within their reach.

- *Greater student engagement.* When students are involved in performance tasks, particularly those that are highly authentic, they are more likely to be highly motivated in their work than if they are answering trivial pursuit-type questions. As a consequence of this engagement, the quality of student work is generally high.

IMPROVED COMMUNICATION WITH PARENTS

Student work produced as part of a performance assessment is extremely meaningful to parents. If collected in a portfolio and used for parent conferences, these products can serve to document student learning (or its lack). If necessary, a student's work may be shown to parents next to that of another (anonymous) student, to illustrate differences in performance. Such documentation may be very helpful to teachers in persuading a parent of the need for additional educational services.

If student work as part of performance assessment is maintained in a portfolio, however, the selections should be made with care. There are many possible uses of a portfolio, and students can benefit from the reflection that accompanies their own selection of 'best work' entries. But as a documentation of student progress, items should be chosen that reflect student performance in all the important instructional goals. For example, if a math program consists of eight strands taught through 12 units, the selections made should document each of the units, and all the strands. These issues will be discussed more fully in Chapter 3 (Making an Evaluation Plan).

A WORD ABOUT GRADING

Many educators ask about converting the results of performance assessment to traditional grades. There are no easy answers to this question for the simple reason that the issue of grading does not lend itself to simplistic approaches. The reasons for this difficulty, however, are not related to performance assessment, but to the varied methods and purposes for assigning grades.

A "score" on a performance assessment is a straightforward matter; student work is evaluated against a clear standard and a judgment made as to where it stands against that standard. If students' grades are also intended (solely) to reflect the degree of mastery of the curriculum, then the score on the performance assessment can be translated in a fairly linear way to a grade. A score of "4" could be an "A," a "3" could be a "B" and so forth.

However, there are several reasons why such a procedure may not be ideal. For one thing, most teachers use other methods in addition to performance tasks to assess student learning. The typical evaluation plan used by a teacher will include tests as well as performance items. Therefore, the results from different methods must be combined in some manner, including weighting some items more than others.

In addition, many teachers incorporate other elements in addition to achievement against a standard into a grade. They may want to build in the degree of progress from earlier work, for example, or the amount of effort or discipline displayed by a student. Alternatively, teachers may have offered some students a lot of coaching in their performance assessments (thereby using them also as teaching tools) and they may recognize that the students' performance reflects more than what they could do on their own.

Therefore, while performance assessments may not translate directly into grades, it may be a good idea to establish some connection between them, making the necessary provision for combining scores on different assessments. If this is done, it sends powerful messages to students. Primarily, such a procedure takes the mystery out of grading, and allows students to know in advance the criteria by which their work will be evaluated. In addition, it also conveys to students that high grades are within the reach of all students. Over time they recognize that if they work hard, they (all of them) can do well. In this situation, good grades are not rationed; all students whose work is at the highest standard can get an "A." As students come to internalize this awareness, and act upon it, it can transform a classroom into a far more purposeful place, and one in which students are concerned with the quality of their work.

SUMMARY

The use of performance assessment conributes many important benefits, beyond strictly measurement issues, to the culture of a classroom. These advantages are derived from clarity of criteria and standards, and benefit teachers, students, and parents.

3

MAKING AN EVALUATION PLAN

Designing and implementing performance assessment entails a major investment of time and energy. In order to ensure that this investment is a wise one, and yields the desired benefits, it is essential to work from a plan. How to develop such a plan, and coordinate it with a school or district's curriculum, is the subject of this chapter.

A CURRICULUM MAP

A useful approach to developing an assessment plan for mathematics instruction is to begin with a consideration of goals in the mathematics curriculum as a whole. An assessment plan, after all, should have as its goal the assessment of student learning in the curriculum; it makes no sense in isolation from that curriculum. Therefore, a plan for assessment should be created with the whole curriculum in mind.

MAJOR OUTCOMES, GOALS, OR STRANDS

A good place to start in thinking about the assessment demands of the curriculum is to consider the curriculum's major outcomes, goals, or strands. Most listings of major mathematics outcomes, or listings of mathematics goals by strand are organized, at least loosely, around the standards published by the National Council of Teachers of Mathematics (NCTM) in 1989. These standards have had an enormous and positive influence on the teaching of mathematics, and have caused educators everywhere to think more deeply about what they teach and how to engage their students in conceptual understanding. The NCTM standards are organized in 13 major areas:

- mathematics as problem solving
- mathematics as communication
- mathematics as reasoning
- mathematical connections
- numbers and number relationships
- number systems and number theory
- computation and estimation
- patterns and functions
- algebra
- statistics
- probability
- geometry
- measurement

Most schools and districts now use some variation on the NCTM standards to organize their mathematics curriculum into major strands, or around major outcomes. Naturally, the numbers and number relationships, for example, taught in the second grade are very different from those in eighth grade but the concept is addressed at both levels. The strands provide the unifying themes that are carried through the entire mathematics program.

Some states, through the State Department of Education, have mandated (or highly recommended) mathematics goals or outcomes also derived from the NCTM standards. For example, Pennsylvania has identified seven major mathematics outcomes. These are, briefly:

- numbers and number systems
- estimation, computation, and measurement with the appropriate use of technology
- patterns, functions, and relations
- formulating and solving problems and communicating the results

- algebra and geometry
- charts, tables and graphs
- statistics and probability

Other states, for example California, have also identified major mathematics outcomes, or strands. Local districts then base their broad goals for mathematics education on those they receive from their state. For example, the Norfolk, Virginia, public schools specify the following:

- computation
- estimation
- organizing data
- analyzing problems
- formulating conclusions
- determining logical solutions

These broad goals, outcomes, or strands provide the framework for curriculum planning. They do not comprise a curriculum; that is developed from the outcomes for each grade level. But they do offer guidance for those preparing the curriculum at each stage.

TOPICS OR UNITS

What students work on every day, and the way in which most mathematics textbooks are organized, is a series of topics or units, rather than outcomes or strands. For example, in a typical seventh grade mathematics text, the chapters concern:

- addition and subtraction expressions
- multiplication and division expressions
- multiplication and division of decimals
- graphing and statistics
- geometry and measurement
- addition and subtraction of fractions
- multiplication and division of fractions
- integers and rational numbers
- ratio, proportion, and percent
- geometry

- area and volume
- algebra and coordinate geometry
- probability

Clearly, some of the topics fit well with some of the strands. For example, the concepts taught in the "geometry" chapter would address the goals in the "geometry" strand. But some of the other connections are not nearly so obvious. In which chapter, for instance, would one find material related to "mathematics as communication," or "estimation?" If educators are committed to addressing all the goals stated or implied in the NCTM *Standards,* or the equivalent document from their own state or district, then they must match the topics or units they teach with the goals inherent in those standards. The best technique to use for this purpose is a matrix, which is described in the next section. A sample matrix is presented on the next page. (Figure 3.1)

CREATING THE CURRICULUM MAP

Across the top of the matrix are listed all the strands, major goals, or outcomes of the mathematics program. In the matrix provided, the ones listed are those developed by the New Standards Project. Down the left-hand side are listed all the topics or units in the year's curriculum, organized, insofar as can be known, in sequence. Then, for each unit or topic, teachers should consider which of the strands or outcomes the topic addresses, and place an X in the corresponding box.

In some cases, research is needed in order to know where to place the X's. For example, if one of the major strands is estimation, many topics may be used to develop that skill, but some are probably better than others; estimation is probably better suited as a component of computation than of geometry. Furthermore, some textbooks will develop the skill of estimation in the context of one topic, others in another. It may be an empirical question then, which topics may be used to develop which of the outcomes, and can be determined by examining the text in use.

What results from this process is a map of the curriculum,

FIGURE 3.1 CURRICULUM/ASSESSMENT PLANNING GUIDE
MATHEMATICS

Course/Grade _____

Outcomes ⁄ Units or Topics	Numbers and Number Systems	Computation Measurement Estimation & Technology	Patterns Functions Relations	Formulate & Solve Problems; Communicate	Algebra Geometry Probability Statistics	Charts Tables Graphs	Statistics Probability

demonstrating the ways in which the different strands or outcomes are (or can be, given the textbook in use) addressed in each of the topics of the curriculum. No doubt some strands receive heavier emphasis than others. In most texts, for example, "computation" is much more heavily weighed than "patterns and functions."

If the map reveals large gaps in the curriculum, for example, if the curriculum map shows that some of the outcomes are not adequately addressed by the program in use, then some adjustments must be made. It is possible that a given curriculum lacks focus on an entire strand of the NCTM standards e.g., mathematical communication. In that case, educators will have to determine in which topics they could develop that skill. Once determined, they can then add X's to the appropriate boxes. For instance, they could decide to add, to each of their units, an objective and the corresponding instructional activities addressing the issue of student communication of the ideas of the unit, whether it is addition of fractions or measurement. In that way, they would adequately address all the different standards.

SUMMARY

A curriculum map can be used to define which units or topics in a curriculum may be used to help students acquire the knowledge and skills inherent in a state's mathematics framework. The map is created by local educators, using the appropriate framework and their own textbook, through the exercise of professional judgment.

ASSESSMENT METHODOLOGIES

Once the curriculum map has been produced, educators must determine how each of the outcomes and each of the topics are to be assessed. Some will lend themselves to traditional testing while others will require more complex performance assessment.

THE ROLE OF TRADITIONAL TESTING

Many mathematics curriculum goals may be assessed through traditional testing. It is, and will always be, important for students to be able to perform accurate computations, or to solve simple equations. The correct use of algorithms is an important part of mathematical literacy. For all these reasons, educators would be ill-advised to abandon the use of traditional tests as part of their total assessment plan.

However, traditional testing is limited in what it can achieve. As teachers survey the curriculum map they have produced, they discover that some of the X's they have written simply do not lend themselves to a multiple-choice or short-answer test. What kind of test, for example, could one construct that would assess students on their understanding of place value, or the use of patterns to solve a problem in number theory?

Moreover, many educators argue that the use of traditional tests, even in those areas of the curriculum where they would appear to be best suited, can do actual harm. This relates to the fact that some students, and their teachers, confuse procedural knowledge with conceptual understanding. That is, students learn a procedure, an algorithm, for getting "the right answer" with little or no understanding of how or why the procedure works, where it would be useful, or what the algorithm accomplishes. Therefore, they can take a test and solve problems correctly, with poor conceptual understanding. If the assessment procedures used do not reveal that lack of understanding, the students may move along to more complex concepts, ones that build on the previous ones, with an increasingly shaky foundation.

Therefore, while traditional tests may be highly useful in assessing certain aspects of the mathematics curriculum, they should be used with caution, and with full awareness of their limitations.

THE PLACE FOR PERFORMANCE ASSESSMENT

Performance assessment is the technique of choice for evaluating student understanding of much of the mathematics curriculum. When students are asked to complete a task, or when they are asked to explain their thinking, they reveal their understanding of complex topics.

Sometimes performance assessment in mathematics can consist of a small addition to traditional testing. For example, students might be asked to solve a fairly traditional problem, but then be asked to explain why they selected the approach they did. Their explanation will reveal their understanding of the process, or their lack of it, and will also serve to assess their skill in the communication of mathematical ideas.

In addition, the authentic application of mathematical procedures is highly motivational to students. Many students regard the applications problems (word problems) they encounter in most mathematics textbooks with disbelief; their reaction is frequently one of 'who cares?' However, with some thought, most teachers are able to create situations that students in their classes might actually encounter, which require the application of the mathematical ideas included in a given unit. The creation of such a task is the subject of Chapter 5, while the adaptation of an existing task is considered in Chapter 7.

A PLAN TO GET STARTED

The idea of creating (or even adapting) performance tasks for all those areas of the mathematics curriculum for which they would be well suited can be a daunting one. After all, if students as well as teachers are unfamiliar with such an approach it is likely to require more time than planned. And since it is unfamiliar, everyone involved is likely to encounter unexpected difficulties. How, then, should one begin?

In general, one should start small. When just beginning, most teachers find that they can use performance tasks only infrequently, at a rate of 4-6 per year. Such a schedule permits teachers the time to create or adapt their tasks to ensure that they will accomplish their desired purposes, and to evaluate student work carefully. But if only one or two tasks per quarter are administered, then they should be those that have the promise to reveal the maximum information about student understanding.

Once the techniques and practices of performance assessment are well understood, and once teachers and students both have some experience in the methodology, performance tasks may be used frequently. However, even with experience, few teachers will administer more than two or three such tasks per month.

SUMMARY

Based on the curriculum map, educators can create an evaluation plan. This plan will include both traditional testing and performance assessment. As they move to performance assessment, teachers are advised to start small.

4

EVALUATING COMPLEX PERFORMANCE

The major advantage of multiple-choice, matching and true/false tests concerns the ease of scoring them; it does not take long to mark an answer "right" or "wrong." Indeed, this speed and ease of correction is their primary value in large-scale testing programs. Because standardized tests are machine-scorable and consequently, inexpensive to administer, they can provide large amounts of data cheaply to school districts and states.

A student's performance on a multiple-choice or short-answer test may be described in terms of percentages. One student might score 87%, another 94%, still another 68%. But when teachers use other assessment methodologies, the concept of "percent correct" loses much of its meaning. What is 87% of an essay? How good (and in what way) should a skit be to receive a score of 94%?

These are not simple questions, and their answers constitute the heart of performance assessment. But there are answers, and answers that respect the important measurement principles of equity, validity, and reliability. This section, through a non-school example, introduces the techniques of evaluating performance, and then discusses each of the issues raised.

A NON-SCHOOL EXAMPLE

All the principles involved in the evaluation of complex performance may be illustrated by an everyday example: that of going to a restaurant. By reading through this example, readers will address, in a familiar form, all the issues they will encounter in designing systems of performance assessment for classroom use. Moreover, it will be evident that the methods for evaluating performance reflect, at their heart, only common sense.

THE SITUATION

Let's imagine that we are opening a restaurant in your town, and that we are at the point of hiring waiters and waitresses. We know that it is important that the waiters and waitresses be skilled, so we want to hire the best we can find. As part of our search, we have decided to eat in some restaurants already in existence, to see if there are people working in these establishments that we can lure away to our restaurant. Consequently, we are preparing to embark on our search mission.

THE CRITERIA

How will we know what to look for? We must determine the five or six most important qualities we would watch for in a good waiter or waitress. But since our focus here is on "performance," we should list only those qualities that are visible to a customer (such as appearance), and not other qualities which, while they might be important to an employer (such as getting to work on time) are not seen by a customer.

A reasonable list of criteria will include such qualities as: Courtesy, Appearance, Responsiveness, Knowledge, Coordination, Accuracy. It is important to write the criteria using neutral, rather than positive, words. That is, for reasons that will soon become apparent, we should write "appearance" rather than "neat."

These criteria could become, of course, a checklist. That is, we could eat in a restaurant and determine whether our server was courteous, responsive, or knowledgeable, etc. We could answer each of the items with a "yes" or "no," and then count the "yeses." However, life tends to be more complicated than a checklist. That is, a waiter or waitresss is somewhat knowledgeable, mostly accurate, a little bit coordinated.

How do we accommodate these degrees of performance? How can we design a system that respects the complexity of the performance, and which we can use to actually compare two or more individuals? The answer is to create a "rubric," a scoring guide.

THE SCORING GUIDE OR RUBRIC

A rubric is simply a guide for evaluating performance, and is presented below.

FIGURE 4.1 WAITER/WAITRESS RUBRIC

	Level One	Level Two	Level Three	Level Four
Courtesy				
Appearance				
Responsiveness				
Knowledge				
Coordination				
Accuracy				

In the left column are listed the different criteria we have determined are important for waiters and waitresses in our fledgling restaurant. Across the top are four columns for different levels of performance. In this case, there are four levels, and the double line between levels two and three indicates that performance at levels three and four is acceptable, and performance at levels one and two is unacceptable. We could, then, broadly define the different levels as:

Level One: "Very poor," or "Terrible" or "Completely unacceptable"

Level Two: "Not quite good enough," or "Almost"

Level Three: "Acceptable," or "Good enough but not great"

Level Four: "Wonderful," "Exemplary," or "Terrific"

In each box, then, we would write descriptions of actual performance that would represent each level for each criterion. For example, for "coordination" we might decide that an individual at level one actually spilled an entire bowl of soup, or a cup of coffee, or could not handle a tray of dishes; someone at level two spilled a little coffee in the saucer, or let some water spill while filling the glasses; a waiter at level three spilled nothing, and someone at level four balanced many items without mishap.

We could fill in the entire chart with such descriptions, and we would then be ready to go evaluate prospective employees. A possible profile might look like the following:

FIGURE 4.2 COMPLETED WAITER/WAITRESS RUBRIC

Name   Wendy Jones   Restaurant   Hilltop Cafe

	Level One	Level Two	Level Three	Level Four
Courtesy		X		
Appearance				X
Responsiveness			X	
Knowledge	X			
Coordination				X
Accuracy			X	

We would still have to decide, of course, whether to hire this individual. Or whether this individual was preferable to another candidate whose scores were all '3's.' That is, we would have to determine how to arrive at a composite score for each individual, so we could compare them.

Naturally, if we were using this approach not for hiring, but for supervision, we would not need to combine scores on the different criteria; we could use them simply for feedback and coaching. For example, since this individual is, apparently, not very knowledgeable, we could provide assistance in that area. We could then work on courtesy, and make sure that customers feel comfortable around this person. That is, for supervision purposes, the system is diagnostic, and enables us, as owners of the restaurant, to provide specific and substantive feedback on areas needing improvement.

SUMMARY

Creating a scoring rubric for a non-school activity provides an illustration of the principles involved in performance assessment.

MEASUREMENT AND PRACTICAL ISSUES

When we contemplate applying these principles to the evaluation of student performance, we encounter a number of issues which, while not technically complex, must be addressed before this approach can be implemented. It should be borne in mind, however, that most teachers have rubrics in their minds for student performance; they apply these every time they grade a student's paper. However, communication is vastly improved if educators can be explicit about the criteria they use in evaluating student work, and what their expectations are. This need for clarity requires us to address a number of technical and practical issues, which are described below.

THE NUMBER AND TYPE OF CRITERIA

For a given performance, how many criteria should we have? For example, when evaluating a persuasive essay, how many different things should we look for? Should we evaluate organization separately from structure? What about the use of language? Or specifically, the use of vocabulary? Or correct spelling and mechanics? What about sentence structure and organization? Should we consider the essay's impact on us, the reader? Is it important that we are actually persuaded by the argument?

Clearly, some of these elements are related to one another; it would be difficult, in a persuasive essay, to have good use of language independently of the vocabulary used. However, other criteria are completely separate from one another. Unless it is so poor as to hinder communication, a student's inadequacies in mechanics and spelling will not affect the persuasiveness of the argument.

The number of criteria used should reflect, insofar as it is possible to predict, those aspects of performance which are simultaneously important and are independent of one another. They will also reflect the age and skill of the students. For example, with young children or special education students it might be necessary to identify specific aspects of punctuation that are evaluated, i.e., proper use of capital letters, commas, and semi-colons; whereas for high school students these may all be clustered under "punctuation" and can include all aspects of mechanics.

However, when criteria are clustered in such a way that they include several elements, these should be specifically identified. Just as, in the waiter and waitress example, "appearance" might include the person's uniform, condition of the hair and nails, and general grooming, individual criteria should specify what elements are included. For example, "use of language" might include richness of vocabulary, use of persuasive words, and proper use of specialized terms.

The criteria, moreover, should reflect those aspects of performance which are truly most important, not merely those which are easiest to see or count. Thus, a rubric for writing should include more than spelling and mechanics; a rubric for problem-solving should include criteria dealing with the student's thought processes and methods of approach.

A rubric should not include so many criteria that it is difficult to use. On the other hand, it should include every important element. As a general rule, since most people cannot hold more than five or six items in their mind simultaneously, rubrics should not contain more than five or six criteria.

ANALYTIC VS. HOLISTIC RUBRICS

The waiter/waitress rubric developed in the previous section is an example of an *analytic* rubric, that is, different criteria are identified and levels of performance are described for each. Using such a rubric makes it possible to analyze student work as to its strengths and weaknesses.

With a *holistic* rubric, on the other hand, the features of performance on all criteria for a given score are combined, so it is possible, for example, to describe a "level two" waiter, or a "level four" waitress. Such holistic judgments are necessary when a single score, such as on an Advanced Placement test, must be given, and also have a place in classroom use, when general feedback is to be given.

For the tasks included in this book, the rubrics are written and applied holistically.

HOW MANY POINTS ON THE SCALE?

In the waiter/waitress example, we identified four points on the scale. That was an arbitrary decision; we could have selected more, or fewer. Performance on any criterion, after all, falls along a continuum; designating points on a scale represents, to some degree, a compromise between practical demands and the complexity of real performance. However, in deciding on the number of points to use, there are two important considerations to bear in mind:

- *Fineness of distinctions.* More points offer the opportunity to make very fine distinctions between levels of performance. However, scales with many points are time-consuming to use, since the differences between different points are likely to be small.

- *Even vs. odd.* In general an even number of points is prefer-able to an odd number. This relates to the measurement principle of "central tendency," which states that many people, if given the opportunity, will assign a score in the middle of a range. If there is no middle, as on a scale with an even number of points, they are required to make a com-mitment to one side or the other.

However, these considerations apply to rubrics that are constructed to apply to a single activity or type of perfor-mance. For developmental rubrics, a large number of points may be preferable. In a developmental rubric, students' per-formance over an extended period of time is monitored on a single rubric. Used most commonly in Foreign Language classes, such a rubric might define oral language proficiency from the most rudimentary through the level displayed by a native speaker. Every student of the language will perform somewhere, at all times, on that rubric, which might have, per-haps 10 points. A second-year student might be functioning at, say, level "3," while a fourth-year student might be at level "5." Both would have made good progress, and yet would have a distance to go before performing at the level of a native speak-er. For such purposes, a developmental rubric with many points on the scale is extremely useful, since it can be used to chart progress over many years.

DIVIDING LINE BETWEEN ACCEPTABLE AND UNACCEPTABLE PERFORMANCE

It is important to decide at the outset where the line will be between acceptable and unacceptable performance. This activ-ity is at the heart of setting a standard, since teachers thereby communicate to their colleagues as well as their students, the quality of work they expect.

In the waiter/waitress example, the line between accept-able and unacceptable performance was established between levels "2" and "3." This, too, is arbitrary; it could just as well been put between the "1" and the "2." When determining where to place the dividing line, educators should consider several points:

- *Use.* If a scoring rubric is to be used for formative evaluation, it is helpful to identify several levels of "unacceptable," since, in that way, teachers can know quickly whether a student's performance on a certain criterion is close to being acceptable or far away. Such knowledge can guide further instruction. On the other hand, if a rubric is to be used to make a summative judgment only, then it is less important if a student's performance is close to the cutoff point; in this case, unacceptable is unacceptable, without regard to degrees of unacceptability.

- *Number of points on the scale.* If a scoring rubric is constructed with six, seven, or eight points, then the placement of the "unacceptable" line might be different from a rubric with only four points. A five-point scale (while not ideal from the standpoint of having an odd number of points) enables two levels of unacceptable while also permitting finer degrees of excellence, with the upper levels representing "barely acceptable," "good," and "excellent."

- *Developmental vs. performance-specific rubrics.* Clearly, for a developmental rubric, one that defines performance over an extended period of time, there is no need to define the distinction between "acceptable" and "unacceptable" performance in the same manner as for a performance-specific rubric. That is, it may be reasonable for a second-year language student to perform at level "3" on a ten-point scale, whereas such performance would not be good enough for a fourth-year student. In this case, judgments as to acceptability and expectations do not reside in the rubric, but in the use that is made of them in different settings.

TITLES FOR LEVELS OF PERFORMANCE

Closely related to the need to define the cut-off between acceptable and unacceptable performance is the requirement to broadly define the labels for each point on the rubric. For professional use, teachers often use terms like "unacceptable," and "exemplary." Such titles might work even if students (or their parents) will see the rubric, but it should be given some thought. Some educators prefer names like "novice," "emerging," "proficient," and "distinguished." Decisions as to the best headings are matters for professional judgment and consensus.

DESCRIPTIONS OF PERFORMANCE

Descriptions for levels of performance should be written in language that is truly descriptive, rather than comparative. For example, words such as "average" should be avoided, as in "the number of computational errors is average," and replaced by statements such as "the solution contains only minor computational errors." "Minor" will then have to be defined, for example, as an error not resulting in an erroneous conclusion, or an error that was clearly based in carelessness.

GENERIC VS. TASK-SPECIFIC

Constructing a performance rubric for student work takes considerable time, particularly if it is a joint effort among many educators. The issues of time and the desirability of sending a consistent signal to students and their parents regarding standards, are important reasons to try to create generic rubrics. Such rubrics may be used for many different specific tasks that students do.

The areas of student performance that appear to lend themselves best to generic rubrics are such things as lab reports, problem-solving, expository, descriptive or persuasive essays, group projects, and oral presentations. Some of these, such as oral presentations, may even be suitable for several different disciplines. It is highly valuable for students to know that when they are preparing an oral presentation, it will always be evaluated, in every setting, using the same criteria.

However, generic rubrics however, are not always possible or even desirable. The elements of problem-solving, and certainly the levels of acceptable performance are very different for high school sophomores than those for second graders. Similarly, the specific elements of a lab report change as students become more sophisticated and more knowledgeable. So while there are many reasons to construct rubrics as generic as possible — and intra- and cross-departmental discussions are highly recommended — it may not be possible to completely develop generic rubrics, even for those aspects of performance in which students are engaged over a period of many years. There are many tasks, and many types of tasks, which require their own task-specific rubrics.

PROFESSIONAL CONSENSUS

When teachers work together to determine descriptions of levels of performance in a scoring rubric, they may find that they do not completely agree. This is natural and to be expected. After all, it is well documented that teachers grade student work quite differently from one another.

Discussions as to the proper wording of different levels of performance constitute rich professional dialogue. While difficult, the discussions are generally enriching for everyone involved; most teachers find that their ideas can be enhanced by the contributions of their colleagues. Rubrics that are the product of many minds are generally superior to those created by individuals. In addition, if a number of teachers find that they can use the same, or similar, rubrics for evaluating student work, communication with students is that much more consistent, resulting in better quality work.

INTER-RATER AGREEMENT

Closely related to consensus on the wording of descriptions of levels of performance is the matter of agreement on the application of the rubric. The only way to be sure that different individuals agree on the meaning of the descriptions of different levels is to actually apply the statements to samples of student work.

The importance of this issue cannot be exaggerated. It is a fundamental principle of equity and fairness that evaluation of a student's work be the same regardless of who is doing the evaluating. However, teachers very rarely agree completely at the beginning. Occasionally, two teachers will evaluate a single piece of student work very differently, even when they have agreed on the scoring rubric. In those cases, they generally discover that they were interpreting words in the rubric very differently, or that the words used were themselves ambiguous. Only trying the rubric with actual student work will reveal such difficulties.

When preparing rubrics for evaluating student work, therefore, the project is not totally complete until examples of different levels of performance have been selected to illustrate the points on the scale. Called "anchor papers" these samples can serve to maintain consistency in scoring.

Clarity of Directions

Another fundamental principle of fairness and equity concerns the directions given to students. Any criterion to be evaluated must be clearly asked for in the directions to a performance task. For example, if students are to be evaluated for their originality in making an oral presentation, something in the directions to them should recommend that they present it in an original or creative manner. Likewise, if students are to be evaluated for the organization of their data, they should know that organization is important. Otherwise, from a student's point of view, it is necessary to read the mind of the teacher and to guess what is important.

Some teachers find that they can engage students in the development of the rubric itself. Students, they discover, know the indicators of a good oral presentation or of a well-solved problem. While students' thoughts are rarely well enough organized to enable them to create a rubric on their own, their ideas make good additions to a rubric already drafted by the teacher.

There are many advantages to engaging students in the construction of a scoring rubric. Most obviously, they know what is included and can therefore focus their work. But even more important, students tend to do better work, with greater pride in it and greater attention to quality when the evaluation criteria are clear. Suddenly, school is not a matter of "gotcha," it is a place where excellent work is both defined and expected.

COMBINING SCORES ON CRITERIA

Occasionally, it is important to be able to combine scores on different criteria and to arrive at a single evaluation. For example, teachers must occasionally rank students, or convert their judgments on performance to a grade or to a percentage. How can this be done? In arriving at a single, holistic score, several issues must be addressed:

- *Weight.* Are all the criteria of equal importance? Unless one or another is designated as more or less important than the others, they should all be assumed to be of equal importance. Educators should have good reasons for their decisions as to weight, and these discussions can themselves constitute important professional conversations. As an example, we could have determined, in our creation of the rubric for a waiter or waitress, that "knowledge" is the most important criterion and is worth twice the value of the others. Then, our rubric and the points possible from each point, appear on the following page:

- *Calculations.* How should the scores be calculated?

FIGURE 4.3 WAITER/WAITRESS RUBRIC

Name   Wendy Jones   Restaurant   Hilltop Cafe

	Level One	Level Two	Level Three	Level Four
Courtesy Weight = 1		X		
Appearance Weight = 1				X
Responsiveness Weight = 1			X	
Knowledge Weight = 2	X			
Coordination Weight = 1				X
Accuracy Weight = 1			X	

Scores: (score assigned) x (weight) = (criterion score)
criterion score on each criterion = total score
total score / total possible scores = percentage score

Using this procedure for Wendy Jones, her point score would be as follows:

Courtesy: 2 (2 x 1)
Appearance: 4 (4 x 1)
Responsiveness: 3 (3 x 1)
Knowledge: 2 (1 x 2)
Coordination: 4 (4 x 1)
Accuracy: 3 (3 x 1)

Total: 18

On this rubric, the total possible points for each criterion are:

Courtesy: 4
Appearance: 4
Responsiveness: 4
Knowledge: 8
Responsiveness: 4
Accuracy: 4

Total points: 28

Therefore, to calculate a total score, we convert the points received to a percentage of the total possible points. Both the points received and the number of possible points reflect the weights assigned to each criterion. Thus, in our example, Wendy Jones would have received a score of 18, which, when divided by 28 is 64%.

- *Cut score.* What is the overall level of acceptable performance? We have, of course, defined the line between acceptable and unacceptable performance for each criterion earlier. However, now we must determine a score which, overall, represents acceptable performance. We could set it as a percentage, for example 70%, in which case Wendy Jones would not be hired in our restaurant. Alternatively, we could establish a rule that no more than one criterion may be rated at a score below "3." This decision, like all the others made in constructing a performance rubric, is a matter of professional judgment.

TIME

Both for large-scale assessment and in the classroom, teachers know that multiple choice, short-answer, matching, and true/false tests take far less time to score than essay or open-ended tests. It is a relatively simple matter to take a stack of student tests and grade them against an answer key. Many educators fear that using performance tasks and rubrics will consume more time than they have or want to devote to it.

There is some validity to this concern. It is true that the evaluation of student work, using a rubric, takes more time than does grading student tests against a key. Also, the rubric itself can take considerable time to create.

However, there are two important issues to consider, one related to the increasing ease of using performance tasks, and the second related to the benefits derived from their use.

- *Decreasing time demands.* When they are just beginning to use performance tasks and rubrics, many teachers find that the time requirements are far greater than those needed for traditional tests. However, as they become more skilled, and as the rubrics they have developed prove to be useful for other assignments or other types of work, they discover that they can evaluate student work very efficiently, and in many cases in less time than the time required for traditional tests.

- *Other benefits.* In any event, most teachers discover that the benefits derived from increased use of performance tasks and rubrics vastly outweigh the additional time needed. They discover that students produce better quality work, and that they take greater pride in that work. If used as a component in assigning grades, teachers find that they can justify their decisions far more reliably than before they were using rubrics.

"SUBJECTIVITY" VS. "OBJECTIVITY"

One of the most important reservations about the use of rubrics to evaluate student work concerns their perceived "subjectivity" compared to "objective" multiple-choice tests. Such fears, while understandable, are completely unjustified.

First, it is important to remember that the only objective feature to a multiple-choice test is its scoring; answers are unambiguously right or wrong. However, many professional judgments have entered into making the test, and even into determining which of the possible answers are the correct ones. Someone must decide what questions to ask and how to structure the problems. These decisions reflect a vision of what is important knowledge and skill for students to demonstrate, and are based on professional judgment.

Similarly, in the construction of a scoring rubric, many decisions must be made; these, too, are made on the basis of professional judgment. But the fact that they are made by teachers in their classrooms, rather than by testing companies, does not make them less valid judgmentally. In fact, it may be argued that, if well thought out, such judgments are superior to those made by anonymous agencies far from the realities of one's own classroom.

In any event, scoring rubrics to evaluate student work and standardized tests are both grounded in professional judgment; they are absolutely equivalent on that score. In both cases, it is the quality of the judgments that is important, and the classroom-based judgment may be as good as that made by the testing company.

SUMMARY

In using scoring rubrics to evaluate student work, many issues must be taken into consideration. However, these issues, such as the number of points on the scale, or the importance of inter-rater agreement, are primarily a matter of common sense.

5

CREATING A PERFORMANCE TASK

The evaluation plan which results from the analysis of curriculum outcomes and topics (determined in Chapter 3) provides the guidelines needed to actually design performance tasks. As part of that plan, educators will have decided which topics or units lend themselves to the corresponding outcome goals or strands, and will have determined the best evaluation strategy for each. This analysis provides the basis for developing specifications (or requirements) for each performance task.

It is important to remember that a performance task is not simply something fun to do with one's students; it is not merely an activity. While it may involve student activity, and it may be fun, it is highly purposeful. A performance task is designed to assess learning, and it must be designed with that fundamental purpose in mind. In the design of performance tasks, a number of factors must be taken into consideration. These are described in this chapter.

SIZE OF PERFORMANCE TASKS

Performance tasks may be large or small. Large tasks take on many of the characteristics of instructional units, and students tend to derive much benefit from them. Large tasks may require a week or more to complete. They are typically complex and authentic, and require students to synthesize information from many sources. Small tasks, on the other hand, are more like open-ended test questions in which students solve a problem and explain their reasoning. These may be completed in a single class period or less. Naturally, tasks may be of medium length and complexity.

In deciding whether to use performance tasks that are large or small, educators must take a number of factors into account. These are outlined below.

PURPOSE

Teachers should be very clear about their purpose in using the performance task. What do they hope and plan to derive from it? Are their purposes purely those of assessment, or do they hope to accomplish some instructional purposes as well?

- *Small tasks are primarily suitable for purely assessment purposes.* If a teacher has taught a concept, for example the distinction between area and perimeter, and simply wants to know that students have understood that concept, then a small performance task is desirable. Such a task will ask students to solve a relatively small problem, to explain their thinking, and to show their work. However, it will not, in itself, also contain activities to be completed as part of the task. The task itself is designed purely for assessment.

- *Large tasks carry instructional purposes as well as assessment ones.* Occasionally, a teacher will want students to truly learn new content as a result of completing an assessment task. If so, a larger task, spread over a number of days, involving many sub-activities, will accomplish this purpose better than a small task.

- *Large tasks are better suited to culminating assessments than are small ones.* If performance tasks are to be used as culminating assessments, they are better if they are quite large and tap a number of different types of skills. However, if performance tasks are for the purpose of assessing a small part of the curriculum, small tasks are more useful since they can be administered frequently and the results used for adjusting instruction. The purpose of the assessment will be a major factor, then, in determining whether performance tasks should be large or small.

CURRICULUM PRESSURE AND TIME DEMANDS

Generally speaking, when teachers are under pressure to "cover" many topics in the curriculum, and consequently have little time to spend on any one topic, they may find that small performance tasks are all that they have time for. Large tasks, while they include many benefits not derived from small ones, do require lots of time, frequently more than many teachers have to devote to them.

SKILL IN GETTING STARTED

Most educators, when they are just beginning to use performance tasks, are unsure of what they are doing; in such situations it is a good idea to use the "start small" principle. For example, when not sure whether the directions to students on a task are clear, it is better to discover that after the students have spent a class period, rather than a week, completing the task. Less time has been lost and there may well be an opportunity to attempt another version of the same task, or a different task, later.

SUMMARY

The size of a performance task is best determined by its purpose (immediate or culminating assessment, or instruction) and by the time constraints and experience of the teacher. In general, it is recommended that teachers begin their efforts with performance assessment using tasks which are small rather than large. This provides the opportunity to experiment with a new methodology in a way that carries low stakes for success, for both the students and the teacher.

CRITERIA FOR GOOD PERFORMANCE TASKS

There is no doubt that some performance tasks are better

than others. What makes the good ones good? How can teachers, in designing or selecting performance tasks ensure that they are as good as possible? Several important qualities of good performance tasks are described below.

ENGAGING

The most important single criterion of performance tasks is that they are engaging to students; it is essential that they be of interest and that students want to put forth their best effort. This suggests that the questions asked have intrinsic merit so that students don't read the question and respond "So what?" or "Who cares?"

How does one find or create engaging tasks? As with so much else in education, professional judgment is the key. Successful instructional activities can be a good place to begin; most teachers know which activities, or which types of activities, are successful with their students. One of these activities, when adapted to the demands of assessment, might make a good performance task. And when reviewing tasks that others have created, one important criterion to always bear in mind is whether the task is likely to be engaging to students.

AUTHENTIC

Related to engagement is the issue of authenticity. Students tend to be more interested in those situations that resemble "real life" rather than those which are completely divorced from any practical application. In addition, performance tasks that reflect the "messiness" of real life make demands on students that more sanitized situations do not. Other things being equal, it is preferable to design or adapt performance tasks that represent authentic applications of knowledge and skill. Such authenticity requires students to use their knowledge and skill in much the same way it is used by adult practitioners in that field. A "template" to be used for designing authentic tasks is provided as Figure 5.2 at the end of the chapter.

However, authenticity is not always possible. Some important school learning is purely abstract, or makes sense only within its own context. For example, when we want students to demonstrate that they can analyze a character in literature, we must ask them to do that, even though such a task has no exact equivalents in "real life." Furthermore, a student's skill in analyzing a literary character assesses not only how well the student understands the character, but the degree to which he or she understands the structure of the piece of literature of which the character is a part.

Similarly, much of mathematics is highly formal and abstract. And while teachers care that students can apply their mathematical knowledge to practical situations, there is much of mathematics, such as number theory, which is internal to the discipline. But such knowledge must be assessed, and a constructed-response question is preferable to a multiple-choice item. However, such a question will probably not reflect authentic application.

ELICITS DESIRED KNOWLEDGE AND SKILL

A good performance task must assess what we want it to assess. It must, in other words, be aligned to the instructional goals we are interested in. Furthermore, the task should be designed in such a way that a student can complete the task correctly only by using the knowledge and skills being assessed.

We should never underestimate our students in this regard. While most students are not devious, most try to complete a task with as little risk and/or effort as possible. If they see an easy way to do the task, even by short-circuiting our intentions, they may well do it that way. Teachers should attempt, therefore, to create tasks that are as tight as possible, without being unduly rigid.

ENABLES ASSESSMENT OF INDIVIDUALS

Many performance tasks that sound imaginative are designed to be completed by students working in groups. And while such tasks may be valuable instructional activities and are certainly fun for the students, they cannot be used for the assessment of individuals. Assessment, after all, concerns the evaluation of individual learning; a performance task in which the contributions of different individuals is obscured cannot be used for such evaluation.

It is possible, of course, to design a performance task that includes both group and individual elements. For example, a group of students may be given some data and asked to analyze it. However, if the analysis is done as a group, each student should be required to produce an independent summary of what the data shows, and each individual's paper should be evaluated independently.

However, even in such a situation, the information for the teacher is somewhat compromised. When reading the work of an individual, a teacher knows only what that student could produce after having participated in a group with other students. With a different group of peers, that same student might have demonstrated much greater, or far less, understanding.

In general, then, it is preferable to create individual performance tasks if these are to be used solely for assessment purposes. If the goal also includes instructional purposes, then compromises on the individuality of the assessment tasks may be necessary.

CONTAINS CLEAR DIRECTIONS FOR STUDENTS

Any good performance task includes directions for students that are both complete and unambiguous. This is a fundamental principle of equity and good measurement. Students should never be in doubt about what it is they are to do on a performance task; the directions should be clear and complete. That does not mean that the directions should be lengthy; on the contrary, shorter directions are preferable to longer ones.

Secondly, the directions should specifically ask students to do everything on which they will be evaluated. For example, if one of the assessment criteria for a mathematics problem involves the organization of information, students should be specifically instructed to "present their information in an organized manner," or some such wording.

Related to the question of directions is that of scaffolding, that is, how much support should students receive in accomplishing the performance task? For example, in a mathematics problem that involves a multi-step solution, should the students be prompted for each step, or is that part of the problem? The answer to this question relates to the purposes of the assessment, and the age and skill level of the students. Less scaffolding is more authentic than more scaffolding; most problems are not presented to us with an outline of how to solve them. In general it is preferable to provide students with problems, with no scaffolding, that represent the optimal challenge for them to determine the proper approach on their own. An intermediate position is to present the problem, with no scaffolding, and then offer "tips" to the student to consider if desired. These tips can contain suggestions that, if followed, would provide guidance as to a possible approach to the problem.

SUMMARY

Good performance tasks share a number of important criteria. These should be borne in mind as tasks are designed.

THE DESIGN PROCESS

Now that the criteria for a performance task are clearly in mind, it is time to create one. What process should be followed? While there are several possible approaches, an effective one is described below.

CREATE AN INITIAL DESIGN

With the specifications and criteria in mind, create an initial draft of a performance task to assess a given combination of student understanding and skill. This task may be created using the format provided as Figure 5.1 at the end of the chapter, and it may, if authenticity is desired, follow the "template" offered in Figure 5.2. This initial draft should be considered as just that, an initial draft; it will almost certainly be revised later in the process.

Obtain Colleague Review

If possible, persuade one or more colleagues to review your work. These may be teachers who work in the same discipline as you or with the same age students, or they may be teachers with very different responsibilities. Both approaches have their advantages and their drawbacks.

Teachers with different responsibilities are more likely to catch ambiguity or lack of clarity in the directions to students than are teachers who are as expert in the field as you are. On the other hand, expert colleagues are better able to spot situations in which the task is not completely valid, that is, situations in which students would be able to complete the task successfully without the desired knowledge and skill. Therefore, a colleague review that includes a combination of content experts and non-experts is ideal.

Pilot Task with Students

Not until a performance task is tried with students is it possible to know whether it can accomplish its desired purpose. Only then can teachers know whether the directions are clear, whether all elements are properly requested, and whether the task truly elicits the desired knowledge and skill. Piloting with students is also the only way to know the degree to which the task is engaging to students.

Students are likely to be extremely honest in their reaction to a performance task. While it is possible to collect their feedback formally, it is generally evident, from their level of engagement and the quality of their responses, whether the task is a good one or not.

Revise Performance Task

As a result of the colleague review and the pilot with students, the draft task will, no doubt, require some revision. This revision might be a major rewrite. More likely, it will be a minor revision in order to make the task clearer, less cumbersome, or differently slanted.

Once revised, the task is ready for the formal process of rubric design discussed in Chapter 6. However, teachers should be aware that the task may need further revision after the scoring rubric is written; that exercise frequently reveals inadequacies (usually minor) in the task itself.

SUMMARY

The process of task design has several steps, all of which should be completed. A performance task should not be used for actual assessment until it has been piloted with students. This suggests that at least a year will elapse between the decision to embark on a program of performance assessment and the implementation of such a system.

FIGURE 5.1 PERFORMANCE TASK DESIGN WORKSHEET

Course _____ Topic _____

Outcome(s) _____

_____

Task Title

Brief description of the task (what students must do, and what product will result):

Directions to the students:

Criteria to be used to evaluate student responses:

FIGURE 5.2 PERFORMANCE TASK. AUTHENTIC SIMULATION

Outcome: _____

Topic: _____

You are (student or adult role or profession)

Who has been asked by (audience or superior)

To (accomplish a specific task)

Using (resources)

Under the constraints of (as found in such a situation)

Your work will be judged according to (criteria)

(Attach a rubric)

Based on Worksheets from the High Success Network and CLASS

6

CREATING A RUBRIC

In order to use a performance task to evaluate student learning, a guide for evaluating student work, such as a rubric, is needed. The development of the task and the application of the rubric should be considered an iterative process (as each is developed and used, it suggests changes in the other) with the final combination of task and rubric evolving over time. This section includes guidance for the design of a rubric for a task.

DRAFTING A SCORING RUBRIC

Generally speaking, the criteria to be used in evaluating student work will have been identified in the course of developing a performance task. However, in order to convert these criteria into an actual scoring rubric, they must be elaborated and further defined. While holistic rubrics have their uses (e.g., in the summative evaluation of student work for awarding a diploma), this section will focus on the design of analytic rubrics. A general format for developing a rubric is provided in Figure 6.1.

GENERIC OR TASK-SPECIFIC?

The first question to be answered concerns the degree of task-specificity of the rubric. If, for example, the rubric is being developed for a group mathematics project, could the same rubric be used for other projects, or is its use confined to this particular one? Indeed, could the elements of the rubric,

FIGURE 6.1 PERFORMANCE RUBRIC

Criteria	(Activity)			
	1	2	3	4

concerned with making a group presentation, be used for other disciplines as well? Are there enough similarities between group presentations for mathematics, science, and social studies that the same evaluation guide could be used for all of them?

In general, of course, generic rubrics are more useful that task-specific ones. Creating rubrics is time-consuming and the more broadly they may be applied, the more useful and powerful they are. However, sometimes a common rubric will have to be adapted for use in other situations and in other disciplines; while many of the elements are the same, the ways in which they appear in student work are sufficiently different to warrant independent consideration.

TASK OR GENRE SPECIFIC, OR DEVELOPMENTAL

Another important question to be considered when creating a rubric is whether the rubric will be used on a single task (or a single type of task) or whether it will be used developmentally with students as they progress through many years of school. That is, will the rubric under development for a mathematics project, be applied for only this particular project which students do in the fourth grade, or could it be used also with students throughout the district, including those in the middle school as well as in high school?

If the rubric is to be used developmentally, it will probably have many more points on it, and the criteria may be written differently than if the rubric is to be used for a single task. A developmental rubric is useful for a school in which students have mathematics portfolios, and may be helpful in charting progress over time. However, a developmental rubric may not be as useful for any particular task as one created specifically for that task.

DETERMINING CRITERIA

Once the question of task-specificity or developmental rubric has been answered, the most important single step in creating a scoring rubric is to identify the criteria to be evaluated. The importance of attending carefully to this step cannot be overstated. It is in the determination of criteria that educators define important aspects of performance, and define, both for themselves and their students, what they mean by good quality. When defining criteria, several issues should be considered.

- *Type of criteria.* In mathematics, an essential criterion almost always concerns mathematical accuracy. Is the answer correct? Are computational errors major or minor? Are answers correctly labeled? Are all possible answers found?

  But in addition to computational accuracy, what else is important? What about conceptual understanding? Do students reveal, either through their approach to the problem or through the errors they make, that they have no understanding of the underlying concepts? Does the problem require a plan? If so, have students organized their information? Have they approached the problem in a systematic manner? Is the work presented neatly? Can a reader follow the student's line of reasoning?

In addition, a mathematics project might require that students collaborate together. How successfully do they do this? Do they establish a good division of labor, or do one or two students dominate the group? If the students make a presentation as part of the project, do they explain their thinking clearly? Are the other students interested in the presentation? Can they follow it? Is it engaging? It is important that the criteria identified for a task not consist only of those that are easiest to see, such as computational accuracy. The criteria should, taken together, define all the aspects of exemplary performance, even if some of them are somewhat challenging to specify and to evaluate.

One successful approach to the identification of criteria is to consider the task and to imagine an excellent student response to it. What would such a response include? The answer to that question can serve to identify important criteria. Alternatively, many teachers do the task themselves prior to assigning it to their students, creating, in effect, an exemplary response, and appreciating the issues inherent in the task for students.

- *Number and detail of criteria.* There is no single best answer to the question of "how many criteria?" Clearly, all important aspects of performance should be captured in the criteria. Moreover, those aspects of performance that are independent of one another should be designated as separate criteria.

It is possible to designate too many criteria, and for them to be too detailed. The resulting rubric is then cumbersome and time-consuming to use. On the other hand, a rubric that is too economical may not provide adequate information to students for them to improve performance. The number and level of detail of the rubric then, is partly a matter of how it is to be used and the age and skill level of the students. Rubrics used with special needs students, for example, are often made in great detail, so both teachers and students are aware of where improvement efforts should be focused.

- *Sub-criteria or elements.* Sometimes, several criteria are related to one another or one may be considered a sub-category of another. In that case, the criteria may contain within them sub-criteria or elements. For example, if students make a presentation as part of the mathematics project, the overall criterion might be "quality of presentation" with sub-criteria of "clarity," "originality and energy," and "involvement of all group members."

Occasionally, when educators think critically about the qualities they would look for in good student performance, they recognize that the task, as written, does not elicit those qualities; they then return to the task and alter the student directions. That is, students could do the task and not demonstrate the criteria that have been defined. In that case, the directions must be rewritten, or the task restructured, to elicit the desired performance.

NUMBER OF POINTS

The question of the number of points on a scoring scale is closely related, of course, to whether the rubric is task-specific or developmental. If developmental, it will almost certainly have more points than if it is task-specific, and the number of points should reflect the age range over which the rubric will be applied. For a skill, such as problem-solving or graphing, that develops from kindergarten through 12th grade, a scale with 10 points would be reasonable.

But even for task-specific rubrics, educators must decide on the number of points. As explained previously, an even number is preferable to an odd number, since it prevents the phenomenon known as "central tendency." But beyond that, there are several considerations to keep in mind.

- *Detail in distinctions.* With a larger number of points on a scale, fine distinctions are required when evaluating student work. While such detail can provide finely-tuned feedback to students, a rubric with many points is cumbersome and time-consuming to use. For practical purposes, a rubric with 4-6 points is recommended. The ones in this collection all contain four points.

- *Dividing line between acceptable and unacceptable performance.* It is helpful, at the outset, to determine the dividing line between acceptable and unacceptable performance. On a four-point scale, this line is either between the "1" and the "2" or between the "2" and the "3." That placement will be determined by where the greater detail is the more useful; that is, is it more useful to be able to specify degrees of inadequacy or degrees of adequacy?

- *General headings for different points.* The different points on the scale may be called simply by their numbers. On a four-point scale then, they would be 0, 1, 2, and 3 or 1, 2, 3, and 4. Or, they could be 10, 20, 30, and 40. Alternatively, the points can be given names such as "novice," "proficient," "exemplary," "great!" If this approach is taken, it is preferable to use positive, supportive words (such as "emerging") rather than negative ones (such as "inadequate").

DESCRIPTIONS OF LEVELS OF PERFORMANCE

Once the criteria and the number of scale points have been determined, it is time to actually write the descriptions of performance levels. Again, this step is critical and includes a number of factors.

- *The language used.* The words used to specify the qualities of different levels of performance should be descriptive, rather than comparative. For example, words such as "average" should be avoided. The descriptions of performance levels serve to further define the criteria, and are further defined themselves only when accompanied by actual samples of student work, called anchor papers.

- *All sub-criteria or elements defined.* If the criteria contain sub-criteria within them, each of these elements should be described in each of the performance descriptions. For example, if a criterion on presentation includes accuracy and originality, and involvement of all group members, then the descriptions for each of the levels should describe the group's presentation with respect to all those elements.

- *Distance between points.* To the extent possible, the distance between the points on a scale should be equal. That is, the distance between a "3" and a "4" should not be much greater than that between a "2" and a "3."

- *The line between acceptable and unacceptable performance.* Placement of the line between acceptable and unacceptable performance should receive particular scrutiny. While the highest and lowest levels of performance are the easiest to describe, those in the middle, that define acceptable and unacceptable performance, are the most important. It is here, after all, that educators define their standards and specify the quality of work on which they insist and expect mastery. It is recommended that this level be described with particular care.

SUMMARY

The most critical step in the development of a scoring rubric for evaluating student performance is its initial design. For this process, a number of factors — such as whether it is generic or specific, the actual criteria, the number of points on the scale, and the language used to define the points — must be taken into account.

PILOTING THE RUBRIC WITH STUDENT WORK

The proof of a rubric is in its use with student work, and not until a rubric is used to evaluate actual student work will its authors know whether it is viable. Several steps are recommended.

EVALUATING A SAMPLE OF STUDENT WORK

A good place to begin is to collect a small number of samples (about 8) of students' work, representing the full range of probable responses in the class. The sample should include those students from whom the best work would be expected, as well as those whose work might not be adequate. If possible, the pieces of work should be anonymous; they could be numbered and referred to by their numbers.

Then, with the rubric in hand, evaluate the student work using the draft rubric. The form shown in Fig. 6.2 may be used, with the criteria listed (or numbered) down the side, and the levels of performance for different students specified in the column corresponding to each one. Surveying the entire page then, provides a summary of the levels of performance represented by the class as a whole, and can offer guidance as to the next instructional steps that may be needed.

FIGURE 6.2 PERFORMANCE ASSESSMENT EVALUATION RESULTS

Evaluator _____ Date _____

Task _____ Grade Level _____

Student / Criteria	Student 1	Student 2	Student 3	Student 4	Student 5	Student 6	Student 7	Student 8

INTER-RATER AGREEMENT

Even with careful design, it is possible that the rubric or the use of the rubric, is not yet reliable. The only way to check this is to request assistance from a colleague. It is recommended that another educator be introduced to the task and the rubric, and be provided with the same sample of student work initially used. This person should then evaluate the same students, and assign scores on each criterion based on the draft rubric.

Scores for each student on each criterion should then be compared. Clearly, the goal is for all scores to be the same, although this is unlikely to occur. Any discrepancies should then be discussed until the cause of the discrepancy is understood; most frequently, discrepancies are caused by a lack of clarity in the words used in the performance levels.

REVISING THE RUBRIC (AND POSSIBLY ALSO THE TASK)

As a result of evaluating student work and of comparing scores assigned with those of another educator, it is likely that the rubric (and possibly also the task) will require some revision. With luck, these revisions will not be extensive and will serve to clarify points of ambiguity.

LOCATING ANCHOR PAPERS

As a final step in rubric design, samples of student work that represent different points on the scale on each of the different criteria should be identified. By keeping these from year to year, it is possible to chart the course of general improvement of student work over time. In addition, only through the use of anchor papers can educators be sure that their standards are remaining the same, and are not subject to a gradual drift.

SUMMARY

Not until a scoring rubric has been piloted with actual student papers will its designers know whether it will prove to be effective.

INVOLVING STUDENTS IN RUBRIC DESIGN AND USE

Many educators find that one of the most powerful uses of performance tasks and rubrics is to engage students actively in their design and use. That aspect of work with rubrics is described in this section, which may be used productively even with elementary students.

ADVANTAGES

Many advantages are cited for engaging students in the design of scoring rubrics. First and most important, by participating in the design of a scoring rubric, students are absolutely clear on the criteria by which their work will be evaluated. Furthermore, many teachers discover that students have good ideas to contribute to a rubric; they know, for example, the characteristics of an exemplary mathematics project.

But more importantly, when students know at the outset the criteria by which their work will be evaluated, and when they know the description of exemplary performance, they are better able (and more motivated) to produce high-quality work. The rubric provides guidance as to quality; students know exactly what they must do.

Consequently, many teachers find that when they involve students in the use of scoring rubrics, the quality of student work improves dramatically. So, when teachers have anchors (e.g., exemplary projects from a previous year) to illustrate good quality work to students, the general standard of work produced improves from year to year.

A PLAN FOR ACTION

It is not obvious just how to engage students in designing and using scoring rubrics for evaluating student work. Some suggestions are offered here.

- *Starting with a draft.* A discussion with students about scoring rubrics should begin with a draft rubric already prepared by the teacher. The teacher should have some ideas, at least in general terms, of the criteria that should emerge from the discussion. Then, while students may suggest original ideas, the teacher can be sure that the final product includes all important aspects of performance.

Students may be asked to contribute both to the generation of criteria and to the writing of performance descriptions. Many teachers are pleasantly surprised with the level of sophistication demonstrated by their students in this endeavor.

The teacher should maintain control of the process of rubric design. While students will have excellent ideas, which should be accommodated to the maximum extent possible, the teacher should never relinquish control of the project to students.

- *Student self-assessment.* The first type of student use of a scoring rubric should be for students to evaluate their own work. Most teachers find that their students are, generally speaking, quite hard on themselves, in some cases more so than their teachers would be. Of course, clear performance descriptions will help in keeping evaluations consistent, but students frequently reveal a genuine concern for maintaining high standards, even when evaluating their own work.

- *Peer assessment.* When the climate in a class is sufficiently supportive, students may be able to engage in peer assessment. Such an activity requires a high level of trust among students. However, if students have participated in the design of a scoring rubric, and have used it to evaluate their own work, they will generally be able to provide feedback to their peers in the same spirit of caring and support. When that occurs, the classroom becomes transformed into a true community of learners.

SUMMARY

The most powerful use of scoring rubrics derives from engaging students in their design and use. However, such participation by students is likely to evolve over time.

7

ADAPTING EXISTING PERFORMANCE TASKS AND RUBRICS

Frequently, much time and effort may be saved by adapting an existing task, with its scoring rubric, to one's own use. Through this approach, educators can benefit from the work of others, and still have a task that reflects their own unique needs.

There are many sources of existing performance tasks that may be adapted, in addition to those in this book. Many textbook publishers now offer some performance tasks and rubrics as part of their package. Some state departments of education have also created prototype tasks. And the National Council of Teachers of Mathematics (NCTM) has published some examples. The techniques for adapting existing tasks are described in this section.

MATCHING OUTCOMES, TOPICS, AND STUDENTS

The first step in identifying tasks suitable for adaptation is to match the outcomes and topics assessed by the task with those in one's own curriculum. The performance tasks in this book have been aligned with the strands developed by the New Standards Project, and with different topics found in most mathematics curricula. By examining those alignments, educators can determine whether a given task would be of value to them in assessing student mastery of their own curriculum.

It is unlikely that such a match will be perfect. Frequently, a performance task will ask students to perform an operation or complete an activity that students in a given class have not yet learned. Alternatively, a scoring rubric will include criteria that do not reflect a district's curriculum. In those cases, either the task or the rubric will have to be adjusted.

Also, a particular task might have been developed with students in mind who are very different from one's own class. In order for a task to be effective, it must be one that students can relate to.

SUMMARY

In order to determine whether a performance task can be used as written, educators must match the task's outcomes and topics with those in their curriculum, and consider their own students.

ADJUSTING THE TASK

The actual task may need adaptation, either to reflect a school's curriculum, to make it more meaningful and relevant to the students concerned, or to adjust the situation to local conditions. Each of these situations will be considered separately in this section.

TO REFLECT A SCHOOL'S CURRICULUM

If there is poor alignment between a performance task and a school's curriculum, the task must be adjusted to correct the mismatch. Such an adjustment will take the form of adding to or subtracting from, or simply changing, the requirements for the students. For example, a particular task might require students to find an average of a group of numbers as one step in solving a problem. If students in a particular class have not yet learned how to do that, the task should be adjusted so that such a step is not needed.

Alternatively, one school's curriculum might teach estimation in the course of work in measurement, while a performance task involving measurement does not, as written, ask the students to estimate their answer before measuring and calculating. In that case, adapting the task might involve adding a step which requires the students to estimate.

TO REFLECT A GROUP OF STUDENTS

Sometimes a task is designed with the characteristics of a group of students in mind, and it is not ideally suited to others. Different classes of students are not identical in the sophistication of their thinking, and in the knowledge and skills they bring to a class. Therefore, a performance task that is to be used with any group of students must be considered with the characteristics of that class in mind.

This factor will often be reflected in the amount of scaffolding provided to students as they solve problems. For lower-functioning students, a task might have to be written with more "tips" for solution than would be needed for more advanced students. Alternatively, a single task might be broken into several sub-tasks that students work on separately.

On the other hand, a task can be made more difficult and cognitively complex. A task that asks students simply to find an answer can be adjusted to require, in addition, an explanation of why a certain approach was employed. Or, a task that includes many suggestions for students as to how to proceed could be rewritten with just the question, with few or no "tips" to the student. Each of these efforts will make the task more challenging, and may make it suitable for an advanced group of students.

If a performance task is adjusted to reflect a group of students, particularly if it is deliberately made more or less challenging, it should be adapted purposefully and the changes noted when student progress is monitored. If, for example, a task is deliberately simplified for a group of students, it should be clear to any reader of those students' records that the curriculum outcomes on which they were evaluated were somewhat different from those of another group of students.

TO ENHANCE ITS RELEVANCE

Another type of adaptation that might be warranted is that which makes a performance task more suitable to a local situation, and therefore more relevant and meaningful to a group of students. For example, a task might ask students to calculate the amount of money they could earn by recycling their household cans, bottles, and plastic containers. If, however, steel cans and plastic cannot be recycled in a particular area, it might be a good idea to revise the task so it concerns only aluminum cans and glass bottles.

Alternatively, an entire situation might be changed to reflect local conditions. For instance, a performance task might concern calculating the floor area of a school's classrooms for the purpose of recommending the purchase of carpeting. If, however, the school is about to have all its walls painted, the students could make those calculations instead, and actually make a presentation of their findings to the maintenance department of the school district. Such efforts to enhance relevance and authenticity pay big dividends in enhancing student engagement in the task.

SUMMARY

A performance task may be adjusted to make it more reflective of the school's curriculum, or more suitable to a group of students, or to reflect conditions in a particular setting.

ADJUSTING THE RUBRIC

If a task is adjusted to reflect a district's curriculum, to be more suitable to a group of students, or to be made more relevant, the rubric will probably also require adaptation. The extent to which such adaptation is needed will depend, of course, on the amount of adjustment to the task itself.

ADAPTING THE CRITERIA

If the task is changed, the criteria may no longer apply. The task may now encourage students to exhibit knowledge, skill, or understanding that were not part of the original task. If so, criteria related to these features should be added. Alternatively, elements of the original task may have been dropped; if so, the criteria corresponding to those elements should be eliminated.

ADJUSTING THE PERFORMANCE DESCRIPTIONS

When a task is changed, particularly if the evaluation criteria are also changed, the performance descriptions may require adjustment. Occasionally, the performance descriptions need adjustment even with no change in the task itself.

- If the level of difficulty of a task has been changed, either by altering the cognitive demands of the directions or by splitting it into several discrete tasks, the performance descriptions for even the same criteria may no longer be suitable. The descriptions may require revision to reflect the changed demands of the revised task.

- Even if the task has not been changed, but is being used with students who are more or less advanced than those for whom it was designed, the performance descriptions may need revision. Sometimes this can be accomplished by simply shifting the descriptions one place to the right, or the left; that is, the description that was a "3" is now a "2," that which was a "4" is now the "3," and a new description is written for the "4."

- If the task has been revised to reflect a particular situation (for example, calculating floor area for carpeting instead of wall area for paint), the performance descriptions may need revising to reflect the changes. On the other hand, they may not need revision, depending on how they were written in the first place. Clearly, the more generic they are, the less revision will be needed. But if the rubric has been written to be highly task-specific, substantial changes will be needed to reflect a different context.

SUMMARY

If a performance task is adjusted to make it more suitable for a group of students, its scoring rubric will almost certainly require a parallel change. Even if the task is not changed, educators may find that they want to adjust the rubric to better match the skills of their students, or the criteria important to them.

PILOTING WITH STUDENTS

No adaptation of a performance task and its rubric is complete without trying it with students. Generally, all performance tasks (even those that are not adaptations of existing tasks) are revised somewhat after this pilot; certainly the scoring rubrics are revised in light of actual student work. The questions to be answered as a result of this pilot are summarized below.

ENGAGEMENT AND AUTHENTICITY

Are students engaged in the task? In the course of revision, did the task become irrelevant and boring to students? If possible, does the task reflect authentic applications of knowledge and skill?

ELICITING DESIRED KNOWLEDGE AND SKILL

Does the task, as revised, elicit the desired knowledge and skill from students? Occasionally, when tasks are revised, they lose their essential nature, so students complete the task without demonstrating the critical knowledge and skill about which their teachers are interested. This is most likely to happen if the student directions have been substantially revised.

CLARITY OF STUDENT DIRECTIONS

Are the directions to the students clear? In particular, if student's work will be evaluated according to specific criteria, have students been informed, in some manner, of those criteria in the directions themselves?

INDIVIDUAL ASSESSMENT

Does the task still permit the assessment of individual students? Or have the teachers, in the interests of making the task more relevant to a particular group of students or a unique situation, also introduced group work that obscures the contribution of individuals?

TECHNICAL FEATURES OF THE RUBRIC

Does the scoring rubric, as revised, still meet all the technical requirements described in Chapter 6? Do the descriptions of levels of performance use vivid words, and avoid comparative language? Are the distances between points on the scale approximately equal? Do the criteria reflect the most important aspects of performance?

Only an actual pilot of the revised task will elicit unambiguous answers to these questions. As educators and their students become more experienced in the use of performance tasks, however, this step may be combined with the first actual use of the task to evaluate student learning. That is, the task may be adapted as needed and used with students. Then, if it becomes apparent that the adaptation did not avoid all the pitfalls described above, the actual scores awarded to students can be adjusted accordingly. For example, if student performance is poor, but it becomes clear that the principal reason for the poor performance relates to lack of clarity in the directions, then the teacher's evaluation of student mastery must reflect that difficulty.

SUMMARY

The final step in adapting an existing performance task and rubric is its actual pilot with students. Only then can educators be sure that it accomplishes their desired purposes.

8

HIGH SCHOOL MATHEMATICS PERFORMANCE TASKS

In this section of the book you will find a collection of performance tasks and rubrics aligned to the mathematics standards, and addressing all the important topics in high school mathematics. They are arranged in alphabetical order (by title), with a table at the beginning of the chapter to assist you in locating tasks you may want to assess specific skills and concepts. Some of the tasks include student work, which serves both to illustrate the manner in which students interpret the directions given to them and to anchor the different points in the scoring rubrics.

You may find that the tasks are useful to you as presented. Alternatively, you may find that they can serve your purposes better if you adapt them somewhat. One way of adapting tasks is to incorporate names of people and places familiar to students in your class. This practice is frequently amusing to students, and therefore engaging.

In addition, tasks may be simplified or made more difficult by increasing or decreasing the amount of structure (or scaffolding) you provide to students. When you, the teacher, give guidance to students by outlining the steps needed in a solution, the resulting task is significantly easier (and less authentic.) Similarly, for those tasks that are provided with considerable scaffolding, you can make them more complex by removing it.

Standard Tasks	Number Operations Computation	Geometry Measurement Concepts	Function & Algebra Concepts
Ball Bearings	X	X	X
The Challenger	X	X	X
Coin Toss	X	X	
Columbus Sailed the Ocean Blue	X	X	X
The Endangered Fraction	X		X
The Eyes Have It	X		X
The Ferris Wheel	X	X	X
A Field Trip	X	X	X
Get a Job	X	X	X
In Your Best Interest	X		X
Let's Get Physical	X	X	X
Matrices in Manufacturing	X		X
Mean Salaries	X		X
A Painter's Solution	X	X	X
Penny Wise	X	X	X
Pool Construction	X	X	X
Price Restoration	X		X
A Rectangular Plot	X	X	X
See the Light	X	X	X
Sierpinski Triangle	X	X	X
Take Me Out to the Ball Game	X	X	X

Statistics Probability Concepts	Problem Solving Mathematical Reasoning	Mathematical Skills / Tools	Mathematical Communication
	X	X	X
	X	X	X
X	X	X	X
	X	X	X
	X	X	X
X	X	X	X
	X	X	X
	X	X	X
	X	X	X
	X	X	X
X	X	X	X
	X	X	X
X	X	X	X
	X	X	X
	X	X	X
	X	X	X
	X	X	X
	X	X	X
	X	X	X
	X	X	X
	X	X	X

BALL BEARINGS

MATHEMATICS STANDARDS ASSESSED

- Number and Operation Concepts
- Geometry and Measurement Concepts
- Function and Algebra Concepts
- Problem Solving and Mathematical Reasoning
- Mathematical Skills and Tools
- Mathematical Communication

DIRECTIONS TO THE STUDENT

Ball bearings are one of the few improvements that have been made to the wheel since its invention. They may be of any size and are widely used in the construction of machines so that friction is minimized when these machines are in operation. They are so important that in World War II, the Allies bombed ball bearing manufacturing plants in Germany because they knew that destruction of these plants would paralyze truck and tank construction.

A steel ball bearing is made from a cylindrical slug of steel which is heated and formed into the shape of a ball. What is the radius of the biggest ball bearing that can be made from a cylindrical slug of radius of 2 cm and height of 2.25 cm? Show the equations that lead to your solution, round to the nearest hundredth, and indicate units throughout.

MATHEMATICAL CONCEPT

In order to solve this problem, students must first find the volume of the cylindrical slug. They must then use this volume as the volume of the sphere in order to solve for the radius of the ball bearing.

SOLUTION

The volume of the cylindrical slug is
$V = \prod (2^2)(2.25) \approx 28.27$ cu cm. (Equation 1)

The volume of the ball bearing is also about 28.27 cu cm, so that
$28.27 \approx (4/3) \prod r^3$. (Equation 2)

Therefore, the radius, r, of the ball bearing is about
$\{28.27/[(4/3) \prod]\}^\wedge(1/3) \approx 1.91$ cm

Note: Allow for some variation in the answer due to either elimination of $\prod$ in the solution process or various approximations of $\prod$ that students might use.

RUBRIC

Level 4: This response offers clear and convincing evidence of a deep knowledge of the mathematics related to this task.

Characteristics:
Equations that led to solutions are shown, answer is correct. Units may be missing or answer may not be rounded to the nearest hundredth, but not both.

Level 3: This response offers evidence of substantial knowledge of the mathematics related to this task.

Characteristics:
Equations that led to solutions are shown, answers are correct to an accuracy other than hundredths and units are missing.
Or
Process is correct throughout except that student evaluates Equation 1 incorrectly. This incorrect value is substituted into Equation 2 yielding the incorrect radius.

Level 2: This response offers limited or inconsistent evidence of knowledge of the mathematics related to the task.

Characteristics:
Equation 1 is solved correctly, but the student does not equate the two volumes. That is, Equation 2 is incorrect or missing.

Or

Equation 1 is incorrect because the values of h and r are switched. This incorrect value is substituted into Equation 2 yielding an incorrect radius.

Or

Equation 1 is evaluated incorrectly. This incorrect value is substituted into Equation 2 but this equation is also solved incorrectly and yields a value other than the one which arises from the substitution.

Level 1: This response offers little or no evidence of knowledge of the mathematics related to this task.

Characteristics:
Student states Equation 1 incorrectly and does not equate the two volumes.

Or

Student offers nothing that is germane to the task.

THE CHALLENGER

MATHEMATICS STANDARDS ASSESSED

- Number and Operation Concepts
- Geometry and Measurement Concepts
- Statistics and Probability Concepts
- Problem Solving and Mathematical Reasoning
- Mathematical Skills and Tools
- Mathematical Communication

DIRECTIONS TO THE STUDENT

America experienced one of its saddest moments on January 28, 1986 when the space shuttle Challenger exploded 73 seconds after take-off. All seven crew members were killed including Christa McAuliffe, the first teacher astronaut. President Reagan appointed the Rogers Commission to investigate the disaster. They concluded that the accident resulted from an explosion caused by the combustion of gas which had leaked through a joint in one of the booster rockets. That joint was sealed by a washer-like device called an O-ring. O-ring performance was a large part of the discussion the night before the launch during a three hour conference between engineers, scientists, and public relations people involved in the operation of the space shuttle. It was decided to go ahead with the launch even though some thought that the forecasted temperature for launch time, 31°F, would make the O-rings too hard to form a leak proof seal of the joints of the booster rockets.

a. The data presented in graph A below was a large part of the discussion the night before the launch.

(1) Some thought that the data did not indicate that temperature affected O-ring performance. Why do you think they reached this conclusion? Explain.

(2) Others thought that the data indicated that the launch be postponed until the temperature was above 53°F. Why do

you think they reached this conclusion? Explain.

b. The Rogers Commission was critical of the fact that the data analyzed in making the decision to launch was restricted to the data shown in graph A. The Commission felt that the data that should have been analyzed is that shown in graph B.

(1) After examining the data in graph B, explain why the Commission thought that the data in graph A was incomplete.

(2) Given the data in graph B, would you have recommended launching at 31°F ? Explain.

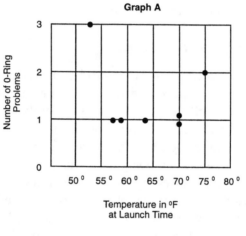

Graph A

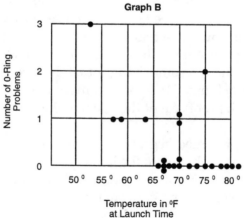

Graph B

MATHEMATICAL CONCEPTS

In order to solve this task students must analyze an incomplete data set and a complete data set. In so doing, they see a powerful example of the consequences of marred data analysis.

SOLUTION

a. (1)   Because the data points are in a U configuration. The greatest number of O-ring malfunctions occurred during the low temperature (53°F) shuttle flight and during the high temperature shuttle flight (61°F). And the lowest number of malfunctions, 1, occurred during shuttle flights which were launched at temperatures between 53°F and 61°F. Therefore, based on the data in graph A, it appears that there is no correlation between temperature at launch time and O-ring malfunction.

   (2)   The data points in graph A show that the greatest number of O-ring malfunctions, 3, occurred at 53°F, and all other launches took place at temperatures above 53°F. There is no data for launches at lower temperatures.

b. (1) The data in graph A does not show the flights with zero O-ring malfunctions and so the complete history of O-ring performance was not considered in making the decision to launch.

   (2) No, because if one considers **all** of the 24 shuttle launches which preceded the Challenger disaster, 17 had no incidence of O-ring malfunction and all 17 were launched at temperatures greater than 66°F.
(According to the Rogers Commission Report: "A careful analysis of the flight history of O-ring performance would have revealed the correlation of O-ring damage to low temperature.")

RUBRIC

Level 4: This response offers clear and convincing evidence of a deep knowledge of the mathematics related to this task.

Characteristics:
Both parts of a and b are answered with convincing justification.

Level 3: This response offers evidence of substantial knowledge of the mathematics related to this task.

Characteristics:
One part of a or b has a weak or vague justification, or is missing, but all else is answered with convincing justification.

Level 2: This response offers limited or inconsistent evidence of knowledge of the mathematics related to this task.

Characteristics:
Two parts of a or b have a weak or vague justification or are missing, but the other parts are answered with convincing justification.

Level 1: This response offers little or no evidence of knowledge of the mathematics related to this task.

Characteristics:
One or fewer parts of a or b are answered with convincing justification.

COIN TOSS

MATHEMATICS STANDARDS ASSESSED

• Number and Operation Concepts
• Function and Algebra Concepts
• Statistics and Probability Concepts
• Problem Solving and Mathematical Reasoning
• Mathematical Skills and Tools
• Mathematical Communication

DIRECTIONS TO THE STUDENT

Suppose that a fair coin is flipped.

a. If the coin is flipped 3 times, what is the probability that
    (1) at least two of the flips are heads.
    (2) At least two of the flips are heads given that one of the flips is a head.

b. If the coin were flipped 25 times, what is the probability that all 25 flips would result in heads? Explain your answer.

c. A game is won if each time a fair coin is flipped it comes up heads. Find the minimum number of flips required for the probability of winning the game to be less than .002.

MATHEMATICAL CONCEPTS

A tree diagram allows students to efficiently organize and visualize the elements of the sample space in part a. The tree can then be read to find the answers to part a, or students may find the answers by applying the laws of probability.

A tree diagram cannot be used to solve part b and so students must find the pattern which will give the number of elements in the sample space no matter how many coins are tossed. Logarithms can be used to most efficiently solve part c.

SOLUTION

a.

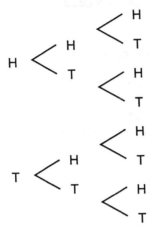

Students may refer to the tree in finding these probabilities or they may find them abstractly using the laws of probability.

(1) There are 8 branches on the tree and three show exactly two heads--HHT, HTH, and THH-- and one shows three heads--HHH. Therefore, the probability is 4/8 or 1/2.

Or

P(HHT or HTH or THH, or HHH) = 1/8 + 1/8 + 1/8 + 1/8 = 4/8 = 1/2.

(2) The tree must be pruned to remove the TTT branch since it is given that there is one head. Therefore, the answer is 4/7 rather than 4/8 as was the case in part (1).

Or

P(At least two heads /one H) = P(HHT or HTH or THH or HHH with TTT eliminated from sample space) = 1/7 + 1/7 +1/7 +1/7 = 4/7.

b. If the coin were flipped 25 times, there would be 2^25 branches on the tree or elements in the sample space. But, only one would show all heads. Therefore, the probability is 1/(2 ^25) or 1 / 33,554,432.

c. If the coin were flipped n times, there would be 2^n branches on the tree or elements in the sample space. Only one would show all heads and the probability of this happening would be $1/2^n$. Therefore, $1/2^n = 1/500 \rightarrow 2^n = 500 \rightarrow n \ln 2 = \ln 500$ $\rightarrow n = (\ln 500)/(\ln 2) \approx 8.96 \approx 9$ flips.

Or, those who have not studied logs may solve this by using a graphing utility to find the intersection of $y = 2^n$ and $y = 500$.

It is possible to take a less efficient approach, arriving at this answer by simply going through powers of 2 until a number greater than 500 is reached.

RUBRIC

Level 4: This response offers clear and convincing evidence of a deep knowledge of the mathematics related to this task.

Characteristics:
All answers are correct and are accompanied by appropriate methods. Minor computational errors are allowable.

Level 3: This response offers evidence of substantial knowledge of the mathematics related to this task.

Characteristics:
All answers are correct but the method is missing or incorrect in one part of the problem. Minor computational errors are allowable.

Or

One or both answers to part a are incorrect due to a flawed tree diagram. Student does not show a tree diagram but the remainder of the task is done correctly. Minor computational errors are allowable.

Or

Part a is correct but the answer to b or c is incorrect or missing but the methods used are appropriate.

Level 2: This response offers limited or inconsistent evidence of knowledge of the mathematics related to this task.

Characteristics:

Two parts are incorrect or missing but an acceptable procedure is apparent in the part that is answered correctly.

Level 1: This response offers little or no evidence of knowledge of the mathematics related to this task.

Characteristics:

None of the answers are correct.

Or

Correct answers appear but there is little or no evidence that they result from acceptable procedures.

Example of a Level 4 Performance

a) 1st toss   2nd toss   3rd toss

[handwritten tree diagram for coin tosses with H and T branches, with ✔ marks]

1) $\frac{4}{8}$ 2) $\frac{4}{7}$

c) 9 times,
see table in
Question b answer.

tosses: 4 5 6 7 8 (9) 10 11 12
options: 16 32 64 128 256 (512) 1024 2048 4096 × 2

The probability would be
one in this done 25
times or

13	14	15	16	17
8192	16384	32768	65536	131072

18	19	20	21
262144	524288	1048576	2097152

22	23	24
4194304	8388608	16777216

25
33,554,432 $\boxed{1/33,554,432}$

This response is scored a 4 because all answers are correct and are accompanied by appropriate methods. Minor errors are allowable. Note that the answer to a (1) was taken from the table (see ✔ marks). Parts b and c are correct and the methods acceptable though not elegant.

EXAMPLE OF A LEVEL 3 PERFORMANCE

a)

(1) $1/2$

(2) $4/7$ (throw out TTT)

b) $\boxed{1/2^{25}} \rightarrow 2.98023^{-8}$

c) $\dfrac{1}{500} \rightarrow \int \left(\dfrac{1}{2}\right)^x = \dfrac{1}{500}$

$\dfrac{1}{2^x} = \dfrac{1}{500}$

This response is scored a 3 because the answer to c is missing but the method used is appropriate. It appears that the student was unable to solve the exponential equation. All other answers are correct and methods are appropriate with the exception of a minor error in part b. The student states the correct answer as a power of 1/2 but does not state the scientific notation for this power correctly.

Example of a Level 2 Performance

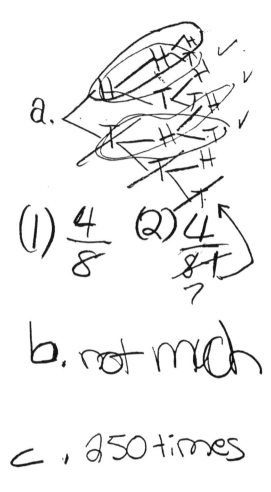

a.

(1) $\frac{4}{8}$ (2) $\frac{4}{8}$

b. not much

c. 250 times

This response is scored a 2 because parts b and c are incorrect but part a is answered correctly with acceptable procedures. The answer to part b shows some intuitive understanding but is too vague to be acceptable. The student shows limited understanding of the concepts involved.

EXAMPLE OF A LEVEL 1 PERFORMANCE

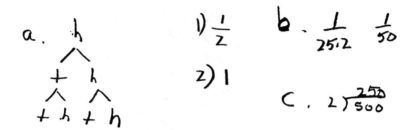

This response is scored a 1 because only one of the answers is correct , a(1), and there is little evidence that the answer resulted from an acceptable procedure (the tree diagram is seriously flawed).

COLUMBUS SAILED THE OCEAN BLUE

MATHEMATICS STANDARDS ASSESSED

- Number and Operation Concepts
- Geometry and Measurement Concepts
- Function and Algebra Concepts
- Mathematical Skills and Tools
- Mathematical Communication
- Problem Solving and Mathematical Reasoning

DIRECTIONS TO THE STUDENT

The first landfall of Christopher Columbus on the shore of a Bahamian island on Friday, October 12, 1492, has had an immense impact on world history. His first voyage to this continent took slightly over 33 days. Columbus sailed a southwestward course from the island of Gomera in the Canaries to an island in the Bahamas. Many historians think that the island upon which Columbus made landfall is Samana Cay. In recent years, the trip from Gomera to Samana Cay has taken modern sailing ships and racing yachts about the same time it took Columbus! Columbus' ships averaged about 3 1/2 knots during the 33 day crossing. (A knot is a speed of 1 nautical mile per hour. A nautical mile is equal to 1,852 meters or about 6,076 feet, and a statute (land) mile is 5,280 feet.)

a. In statute miles, about how far is it from Gomera to Samana Cay? Indicating units of measure throughout, show how you arrived at your answer. Round your answer to the nearest hundred statute miles.

b. If you traveled this distance southwest of your home, where would you be? Show the route on a map and indicate, on the map, the proportion you used to scale the distance.

MATHEMATICAL CONCEPT

Students must use the $d = rt$ relationship and analyze linear dimensions in order to solve the first part of the problem. The second part requires that students measure in a southwesterly direction and use a proportion based on the map's key to locate the place as far from their home as Samana Cay is from Gomera.

SOLUTION

a. $d = rt$ = [6,076ft/nautical mile x 3.5 nautical miles/hr] x [33 days x 24 hrs/day]

      = 16,842,672 ft x 1 statute mile/5280 ft

      = 3189.9

      ≈ 3200 statute miles

b. Answers vary depending upon location of home. Map should show route and scale proportion.

RUBRIC

Level 4: This response offers clear and convincing evidence of a deep knowledge of the mathematics related to this task.

Characteristics:
Student uses correct formula, substitutes correctly with conversions, and arrives at correct answer in statute miles. Answer may be rounded to something other than the nearest hundred or units may be missing--but not both. Student correctly locates a point approximately 3200 miles southwest of their home. Map shows route and scale proportion.

Level 3: This response offers evidence of substantial knowledge of the mathematics related to this task.

Characteristics:
Student uses correct formula, substitutes correctly with conversions, and arrives at the correct answer in statute miles.

Answer may be rounded to something other than the nearest hundred and units may be missing. Answer to b may be vague--locating a general area in which the specific place is located. Map should show route and/or scale proportion.

Or,

Student uses correct formula, substitutes correctly with conversion but arrives at an incorrect answer due to a minor error. Student correctly locates a point, approximately the number of miles indicated by their answer to part a, that is southwest of their home. Map should show route and/or scale proportion.

Level 2: This response offers limited or inconsistent evidence of knowledge of the mathematics related to this task.

Characteristics:
Student uses correct formula, substitutes correctly with conversions, and arrives at the correct answer in statute miles. Answer may be rounded to something other than the nearest hundred and units may be missing. Answer to b is incorrect, or answer is correct but map work is missing.

Or,

Student uses correct formula, substitutes correctly with conversion but arrives at an incorrect answer due to a minor error. Answer to b may be vague--locating a general area in which the specific location is located. Map work may be incomplete.

Or,

Student uses correct formula but misses a conversion--nautical miles to feet, or days to hours, or feet to statute miles. Units may be missing. Student correctly locates a point, approximately the number of miles indicated by their answer to part a, that is southwest of their home. Map shows route and proportion.

Level 1: This response offers little or no evidence of knowledge of the mathematics related to this task.

Characteristics:
Student uses correct formula but misses more than one conversion. Map may be correct or incorrect based on answer to part a.

EXAMPLE OF A LEVEL 4 PERFORMANCE

$$\frac{33 \text{ days}}{} \left| \frac{24 \text{ hrs}}{1 \text{ day}} \right| \quad 792 \text{ hrs}$$

$$\frac{3.5 \text{ knots}}{hr} \left| \frac{6076 ft}{1 \text{ knot}} \right| \frac{1 mi}{5280 ft} = 4.03 \text{ mi/hr}$$

$D = RT$

$D = (792)(4.03)$

$D = 3191.8 \approx 3200 \text{ mi}$

This puts you about 1045 miles off the coast of Mexico

This response is scored a 4 because the student used the correct formula, made each of the conversions, and arrived at the correct answer to part a. In addition, this student correctly located a place which is approximately 3200 miles from their home in New Jersey. Map work was complete and correct.

EXAMPLE OF A LEVEL 3 PERFORMANCE

a. $\frac{34\frac{1}{2}}{}$ =   33 day x 24 hrs - 792 hrs

792 hrs x 3.5 = 2772 nautical miles

2772 nm x 6076ft = 16842672/5280ft

= 3189.9 miles

3200 miles

b. in Pacific ocean

This response is scored a 3 because the student used the correct formula, made each of the conversions, and arrived at the correct answer to part a. In addition, this student gave a vague answer to part b. Map work showed scale proportion only.

EXAMPLE OF A LEVEL 2 PERFORMANCE

$$
\begin{array}{r}
35 \\
\times 24 \\
\hline
54 \\
\times 33 \\
\hline
2,772
\end{array}
$$

$$5285\overline{)6076}$$ 1.2

1.2 mi. per nautical

$$
\begin{array}{r}
2,776 \\
+ \quad 1.2 \\
\hline
3326.4
\end{array}
$$

3,326.4 statute mi.

1,000 west of Hawaii

This response is scored a 2 because the student used the correct formula, made each of the conversions, and arrived at the correct answer to part a, though the answer was not rounded to the nearest 100 miles. However, the student's answer to part b is incorrect.

EXAMPLE OF A LEVEL 1 PERFORMANCE

a) $6076 \cdot 3\frac{1}{2} = 21,266 = d$

b) ??? , maybe Australia ??

This response is scored a 1 because the student used the correct formula, made no conversions, and so, arrived at an incorrect answer to part a. In addition, the student's answer to part b is incorrect based on their answer to part a.

THE ENDANGERED FRACTION

MATHEMATICS STANDARDS ASSESSED

- Number and Operation Concepts
- Function and Algebra Concepts
- Problem Solving and Mathematical Reasoning
- Mathematical Skills and Tools
- Mathematical Communication

DIRECTIONS TO THE STUDENT

Throughout the history of American stock exchanges, stock prices have been quoted in multiples of 1/8 of a dollar or 12.5 cents. This tradition dates back to pre-Revolutionary days when dollar coins could be physically cut into "pieces of eight" to make change. However, foreign stock exchanges price their stock in decimal amounts with pennies being the smallest units in which they trade. American stock exchanges are increasingly under pressure to join foreign markets in decimal pricing.

Answer the following questions, showing the procedures that lead to your answers.

1. Suppose that you bought 10,000 shares of a stock when it was selling at its yearly low of 41 1/2, and that it is now worth 85 7/8.
    a. In dollars and cents, how much did you profit by this increase?
    b. By what percent did your investment increase? (Round to the nearest percent.)
2. Could a stock listed on an American stock exchange sell for $20.78? Explain.
3. Some American exchanges are now allowing for prices to be quoted in multiples of 1/16 of a point. Could a stock listed on such an exchange sell for $20.78? Explain.

4. Name 5 amounts that can be expressed in dollars and a whole number of cents that can be used in exchanges that allow for pricing in multiples of 1/8.

5. Write a rule for every dollar and whole cent amount that represents a selling price on a market which prices in multiples of one eighth? (You may state the rule as an equation or you may express it in words.)

6. Representatives in Congress as well as many financial experts believe that American investors would be better served if our pricing of stock were done as it is in foreign stock markets. Why do you think this is the case? (Keep in mind that the price at which investors can buy stock is more than the price at which they can sell that particular stock to a broker and that difference is calculated in eighths.)

MATHEMATICAL CONCEPTS

This task provides students with an application of mathematics within an historical context. Students will see the difference between calculation in fractions rather than decimals. The simplicity of working in decimals as opposed to fractions should also be apparent to students as a result of performing this task.

SOLUTIONS

1. a. profit = 10,000 x (85 7/8 - 41 1/2) = 10,000 x 44 3/8 = $ 443,750

   b. percent increase = [(44 3/8) / (41 1/2)] x 100 % = 107 %

2. No, since $20.78 is between 20.75 = 20 3/4 = 20 6/8 and 20.875 = 20 7/8.

3. No, $20.78 is between 20.75 = 20 3/4 = 20 12/16 and 20.8125 = 20 13/16.

4. Answers will vary but all must be multiples of 2 and $ .125.

5. Answers should state that prices must be multiples of 2 and .125, or that dollar and cent amount = 2n(.125), where n is a natural number.

6. Answers will vary but the response probably will indicate that a change to decimal pricing will benefit the investor because fractions are easier to work with and/or because pricing increments of single cents means less of a spread than increments of 12.5 cents and this would mean the investor would make more on the sale of stock.

RUBRIC

Level 4: This response offers clear and convincing evidence of a deep knowledge of the mathematics related to this task.

Characteristics:
Answers to each part are correct with correct procedures and explanations.
In addition, the answer to 6 is thoughtful.
Or
An answer may be incorrect due to a minor error. The remainder of the answers are correct with correct procedures and explanations. Answer to 6 is thoughtful.

Level 3: This response offers evidence of substantial knowledge of the mathematics related to this task.

Characteristics:
Answers are correct with correct procedures and explanations but answer to 6 is weak or missing.
Or
An answer is incorrect due to a major error in procedure or a missing procedure. The remainder of the answers are correct with correct procedures and explanations. The answer to 6 may be weak.

Level 2: This response offers limited or inconsistent evidence of knowledge of the mathematics related to this task.

Characteristics:
Answers are correct. However, procedures and explanations are missing for most but not all of the task. Answer to 6 is thoughtful.

Or

Answers to two or three parts of the task are incorrect but procedures or explanations are shown for the parts that were answered correctly. The answer to 6 may be weak.

Level 1: This response offers little or no evidence of knowledge of the mathematics related to this task.

Characteristics:
Answers are incorrect or missing for more than 3 parts of the task.

EXAMPLE OF A LEVEL 4 PERFORMANCE

1. a)

10,000
× 41.5
415,000

10,000
× 85 7/8 .875
858,750
− 415,000
$443,750

b) p × 85.875 = 41.5
/85.875 /85.875
P = .483
↓
48%

6. Because if 3 the spread is less than 12½¢, the investor will make more money on a sale

2. No, because 6/8 of a dollar is 75¢ and 7/8 of a dollar is 87.5¢ and shares are only sold in increments of 1/8.

3. 1/16 = $.0625 .0625) 20.78 = 332.48
No, because 20.78 doesn't divide by 1/16 evenly.

4. 1) 6¼ = 6.25
~~2) 6⅛ = 6.125~~ 7¼ = 7.25
3) 6½ = 6.50
~~4) 6⅜ = 6.375~~ 7½ = 7.50
5) 6¾ = 6.75

5. Selling price must be divisible by .125. (or 1/8)

This response is scored a 4 because the answers to each part are correct with correct procedures and explanations. The answer to part 6 is thoughtful.

EXAMPLE OF A LEVEL 3 PERFORMANCE

1. 85.875
  -41.5
  _____
  44.375
  × 10,000
  _____
  443,750
  Profit

more than 100 percent

2. No 78¢ not multiple of $\frac{1}{8}$

3. Not multiple of $\frac{1}{16}$ either.

4. 38.00, ~~38.125~~, 38.25, ~~38.375~~,
   38.50, ~~38.625~~, 38.75, 39.00

5. Take multiples of .25

6. Decimals are better.

This response is scored a 3 because the answers to all but one part are correct as are the procedures. Specifically, the answer to 1b is vague and the procedure is missing. In addition, the answer to 6 is weak.

EXAMPLE OF A LEVEL 2 PERFORMANCE

1. a. $44.38

   b.

2. No, because "$20.78" is in decimals but the American Stock Exchange is in "eighths."

3. No, it does not come out evenly.

4. $1.25 (1 2/8), $75.50 (75 4/8), $89.75 (89 6/8), $3.00 (3 0/8), $2.50 (2 4/8)

5. It increases by 2/8 ths each time.

6. Because it's easier to work with decimals than 8th. (8/16)

This response is scored a 2 because the answers to two parts are incorrect--1a shows some semblance of understanding but is wrong, 1b was not attempted; and the explanation for 2 is wrong and the explanation for 3 is vague. However, the procedures for the correct answers are apparent and the answer to 6 is thoughtful.

EXAMPLE OF A LEVEL 1 PERFORMANCE

1. a) $85\frac{3}{8} - 41\frac{1}{2} = 44\frac{3}{8}$

   b) More than double

2. Yes

3. No

4. $40, 40\frac{1}{2}, 50, 50\frac{1}{2}, 60$

   $ have to be whole or half
   Because of the U-N.

This response is scored a 1 because the answers to most parts are incorrect or incomplete --1a and b show some semblance of understanding but are wrong; and the explanation for 2 is wrong and the explanation for 3 is vague. In addition, procedures are missing for most of the task.

THE EYES HAVE IT

MATHEMATICS STANDARDS ASSESSED

- Number and Operation Concepts
- Function and Algebra Concepts
- Statistics and Probability Concepts
- Problem Solving and Mathematical Reasoning
- Mathematical Skills and Tools
- Mathematical Communication

DIRECTIONS TO THE STUDENT

Each person inherits **two** genes, one from each parent, which determine their eye color. Each gene is either dominant, type *B* for brown, or recessive, type *b* for blue. There are two ways that a person can have brown eyes: they may either be *brown eyed dominant* which means they have two brown genes *(BB)*, or *brown eyed recessive* which means that one gene is brown and one gene is blue *(Bb)*. But there is only one way that a person can have blue eyes: both of the genes they inherit from their parents must be blue *(bb)*. The gene that a child inherits from a parent is a random choice of one of the parent's two genes.

Show your process in finding the probability that a child has

(a) blue eyes if her mother is *brown eyed recessive (Bb)*, and her father is blue eyed.

(b) blue eyes if her paternal grandmother is *brown eyed recessive (Bb)*, her paternal grandfather is blue eyed, her maternal grandmother is *brown eyed dominant (BB)*, and her maternal grandfather is *brown eyed recessive (Bb)*.

MATHEMATICAL CONCEPT

It is likely that the student will solve this problem by modeling the situation so that complete sample spaces are illustrated. After this is done, determination of the number of possible as well as favorable outcomes is easily calculated.

SOLUTION

(a) Students may show work in the form of a box or a tree diagram, or their work may be abstract.

P(blue eyed child/ *Bb* parent and *bb* parent) = $2/4 = 1/2$ based on the sample space as diagrammed below:

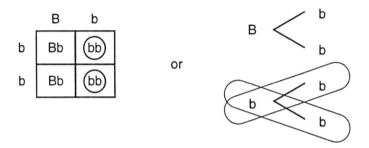

Or P(b from hybrid) x P(b from recessive) = $1/2 \times 1 = 1/2$

(b) There are 16 possible outcomes which arise from the fact that Mom can be BB (p= 1/2) or Bb (p= 1/2), and Dad can be Bb (p= 1/2) or bb (p= 1/2). The probability their child will be blue eyed is 3/16 since 3 out of the 16 possible outcomes are favorable as shown below.

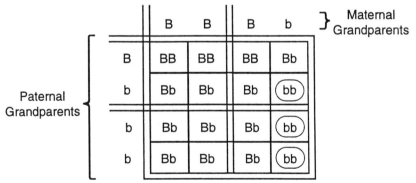

Or P(Father blue eyed) x P(Mother brown eyed recessive) x P(daughter is blue eyed) + P(Father brown eyed recessive) x P(Mother brown eyed recessive) x P(daughter is blue eyed) = (1/2)(1/2)(1/2) + (1/2)(1/2)(1/4) = 1/8 + 1/16 = 3/16.

RUBRIC

Level 4: This response offers clear and convincing evidence of a deep knowledge of the mathematics related to this task.

Characteristics:
Answers are correct and processes for both are viable. Minor flaw is possible.

Level 3: This response offers evidence of substantial knowledge of the mathematics related to this task.

Characteristics:
Answer and process for a is correct. Answer for b is incorrect but process is viable yet incomplete.
Or
Answer and process for a is correct. Answer for b is incorrect but process is viable--more than one minor flaw caused the wrong answer.

Level 2: This response offers limited or inconsistent evidence of knowledge of the mathematics related to this task.

Characteristics:
Answers are correct but processes are incomplete.
Or
Answer and process for a is correct. Answer for b is incorrect or missing but there is evidence of a process which might have lead to the correct answer.

Level 1: This response offers little or no evidence of knowledge of the mathematics related to this task.

Characteristics:
Answer/s are correct but no process is shown.
Or
Answer/s are incorrect or missing, and processes are incorrect or missing.

EXAMPLE OF A LEVEL 4 PERFORMANCE

a.) $Bb^{\female} \times bb^{\male}$

	B	b
b	Bb	bb
b	Bb	bb

1Bb to 1 bb

$\frac{2bb}{4\ total} = 50\% \ chance$

— or —

$Bb^{\female} \times bb^{\male}$

$\frac{1}{2} \times \frac{2}{2} = \frac{1}{2} = 50\%$

↑ 1 b per 2 letters   ↑ 2 b per 2 letters

b.) $Bb^{\female} \times bb^{\male}$

Grandma   Grandpa

FATHER'S SIDE

	B	b
b	Bb	bb
b	Bb	bb

1 Bb : 1 bb

both can work and both have a $\frac{1}{2}$ chance

MOTHER'S SIDE

$BB^{\female} \times Bb^{\male}$

Grandma   Grandpa

	B	B
B	BB	BB
b	Bb	Bb

1 BB : 1 Bb

must be Bb → $\frac{1}{2}$ chance

$Bb \times Bb$

	B	b
B	BB	Bb
b	Bb	bb

$\frac{1}{4}$

$Bb \times Bb$

	b	b
B	Bb	Bb
b	bb	bb

$\frac{1}{2}$

$\frac{1}{4}\left(\frac{1}{4}\right) + \frac{1}{4}\left(\frac{1}{2}\right) = \frac{1}{16} + \frac{1}{8} = \frac{3}{16}$

This student received a score of 4 because the answers are correct and the processes which lead to both answers are viable.

EXAMPLE OF A LEVEL 3 PERFORMANCE

a) Mother: Bb , Father: bb
$\to$ 50% that gene is b $\to$ 100% that gene is b $\therefore \frac{1}{2} \cdot 1 = \frac{1}{2} =$ [50% that child has blue eyes]
($\frac{1}{2}$)   (1)

b) Paternal Grandmother: Bb, Paternal Grandfather: bb
$\hookrightarrow$ The father has a 50% ($\frac{1}{2}$)
chance of being blue eyed (bb)
Maternal Grandmother: BB , Maternal Grandfather: Bb
$\hookrightarrow$ The mother has a 50% ($\frac{1}{2}$)
chance of being Bb
If Father is blue eyed (bb) and mother is Bb then there is a 50% ($\frac{1}{2}$)
chance that the daughter will also be blue eyed.

$$\frac{1}{2} \cdot \frac{1}{2} \cdot \frac{1}{2} = \frac{1}{8} = [12.5\% \text{ that child has blue eyes}]$$

This student received a score of 3 because the answer and process for a is correct; however, the answer to b is incorrect due to a incomplete though viable process. The student clearly understands how to analyze the probabilities but has neglected to consider the case of the father being Bb and the mother being Bb. This scenario would lead to a $1/2 \times 1/2 \times 1/4$ or $1/16$ probability of a blue eyed child. Had this been added to the student's answer of $1/8$, the correct answer would have been calculated.

EXAMPLE OF A LEVEL 2 PERFORMANCE

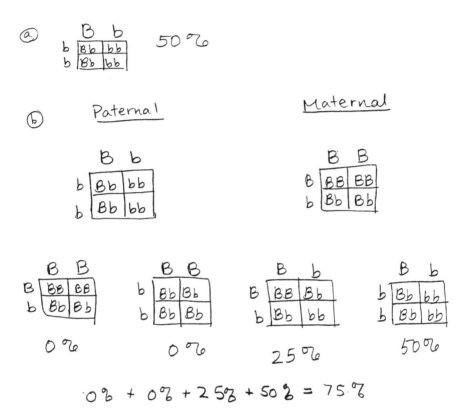

This student received a score of 2 because the answer and process for a is correct; however, the answer for b is incorrect due to the due to misinterpretation of the probabilities indicated by each box. Because of the presence of the boxes which represent all of the possibilities, there is evidence of a process which might have lead to the correct answer.

EXAMPLE OF A LEVEL 1 PERFORMANCE

a) $\frac{1}{2}$ b) $\frac{4}{16} - \frac{1}{16} = \frac{3}{16}$

This student received a score of 1 because although the answers are correct, there is no evidence of the processes which lead to these answers.

THE FERRIS WHEEL

MATHEMATICS STANDARDS ASSESSED

• Number and Operation Concepts
• Geometry and Measurement Concepts
• Function and Algebra Concepts
• Problem Solving and Mathematical Reasoning
• Mathematical Skills and Tools
• Mathematical Communication

DIRECTIONS TO THE STUDENT

The Ferris Wheel, a classic amusement park ride, was invented by George Ferris. Mr. Ferris was an American engineer who debuted his wheel at the 1893 World's Fair in Chicago.

Suppose that you are 4 feet off the ground in the bottom car of a Ferris Wheel and ready to ride. If the radius of the wheel is 25 ft and it makes 2 revolutions per minute,

a. Sketch a graph that shows your height h (in ft) above the ground at time t (in sec) during the first 45 seconds of your ride.
b. Why is your curve periodic? Explain in terms of the problem.
c. What is the period of your curve? Explain this number in terms of the problem.
d. Give a possible equation for your curve.
e. At what speed are you traveling on the Ferris Wheel? (ft/sec) Explain.
f. Suppose that the radius of the Wheel were decreased and that the Wheel still makes two revolutions per minute, would the

(1) period change? Explain. (If yes, indicate if it would increase or decrease.)

(2) amplitude change? Explain. (If yes, indicate if it would increase or decrease.)

(3) speed change? Explain. (If yes, indicate if it would increase or decrease.)

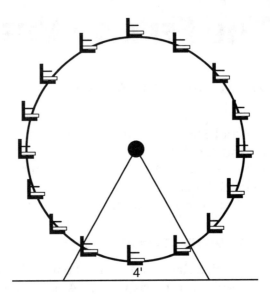

MATHEMATICAL CONCEPTS

Students express the Ferris Wheel's motion as a circular function, and interpret that motion by using their knowledge of periodic functions. This enhances their understanding of circular functions and the meaning of quantities such as amplitude and period.

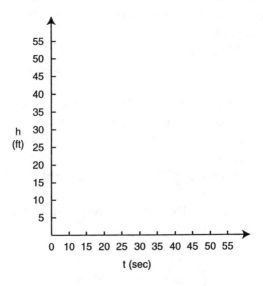

SOLUTION

a. Graph should look like:

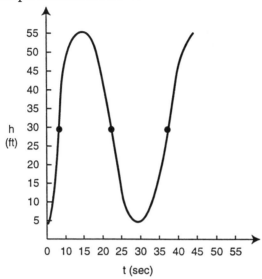

t (sec)

b. The car covers every height from 4' to 54' on the way up and then again on the way down, and this is the case with each revolution.

c. The period is 30 seconds since this is the time for one complete revolution.

d. Using the cosine function, the most likely answers are y = -25cos[(∏/15)x] + 29 or y = 25cos[(∏/15)(x - 15)] + 4. However, there are an infinite number of possible answers which can be generated by replacing x with (x-h) where h = 30n (n is any integer) in the former case, or by replacing x with (x-h) where h = 15 + 30n (n is any integer) in the latter case.

Using the sine function, the most likely answer will be y = 25sin[(∏ /15)(x - 7.5)] + 29. Again, there are an infinite number of possible answers which can be generated by replacing x with (x-h) where h = 15 + 30n (n is any integer).

e. The Ferris wheel makes 2 revolutions per minute, each revolution covers 50 Π feet, therefore, the speed is 100 Π ft / min ≈ 314 ft/60 sec or about 5'/sec.

f.   (1) No, because it would still take 30 seconds to complete a revolution.

(2) Yes, the amplitude would decrease because the height of the wheel would decrease.

(3)   Yes, speed would decrease since the circumference would decrease and so, less distance would be covered per minute or second.

RUBRIC

Level 4: This response offers clear and convincing evidence of a deep knowledge of the mathematics related to this task.

Characteristics:
The graph is correct, and all questions are answered correctly with appropriate explanations. A computational flaw may occur.

Level 3: This response offers evidence of substantial knowledge of the mathematics related to this task.

Characteristics:
The graph is correct, and all questions are answered correctly but one explanation may be weak or missing.
Or
The graph is correct, and one question is incorrectly answered or missing but all else is correct with appropriate explanations.
Or
The graph is flawed but shows a periodic function, and all other questions are correctly answered with appropriate explanations.

Level 2: This response offers limited or inconsistent evidence of knowledge of the mathematics related to this task.

Characteristics:
The graph is correct or flawed but periodic, and most but not all of the questions are answered correctly with appropriate explanations. Explanations may be weak. (More than one question must be incorrect.)

Level 1: This response offers little or no evidence of knowledge of the mathematics related to this task.

Characteristics:
Most of the questions are answered incorrectly or are missing.
                                    Or
Most of the explanations are missing or weak.

A FIELD TRIP

MATHEMATICS STANDARDS ASSESSED

- Number and Operation Concepts
- Geometry and Measurement Concepts
- Function and Algebra Concepts
- Problem Solving and Mathematical Reasoning
- Mathematical Skills and Tools
- Mathematical Communication

DIRECTIONS TO THE STUDENT

A bus company has contracted with a local high school to carry 450 students on a field trip. The company has 18 large busses which can carry up to 30 students and 19 small busses which can carry up to 15 students. There are only 20 drivers available on the day of the field trip.

A) If x large busses and y small busses are used, write a system of inequalities that models all of the information given above.

B) Shade the set of points in the plane that contains all possible solutions to the inequalities asked for in part A.

C) The total cost of operating the large busses is $225 a day, and the total cost of operating the small busses is $100 per day.

   (1) Explain how to use this additional information in conjunction with the graph, asked for in part B, to determine how many busses of each type should be used to minimize the cost of transporting all 450 students. Label all points on your graph that are important to the solution of the problem.

   (2) Determine the minimum cost of transporting all 450 students. Be sure that your work is complete and clear.

MATHEMATICAL CONCEPTS

This is a linear programming problem in which students must model the problem with a linear system, find the feasible region of that system, and minimize cost by testing the vertices of the region. They may use a family of cost lines to find the optimum situation. A graphing utility may be used to help graph the feasible region.

SOLUTIONS

A) $x + y \leq 20$ $x \geq 0$
    $30x + 15y \geq 450$ $y \geq 0$
    $x \leq 18$
    $y \leq 19$

(If, in addition, $x + y \leq 37$ is given that is acceptable and will not change the feasible region)

B)

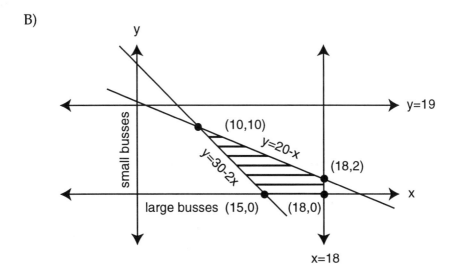

C)

(1) The total cost, C, of operating the busses is C = 225 x + 100 y. The vertices of the feasible region are (10 , 10), (15 , 0), (18 , 0), and (18 , 2). The minimum cost will occur at one of these critical points of the feasible region.

(2) Testing* the critical points in the cost equation yields:
--using 18 large busses and 2 small busses costs $4,250
--using 18 large busses and 0 small busses costs $4,050
--using 15 large busses and 0 small busses costs $3,375
--using 10 large busses and 10 small busses costs $3,250

Therefore, the most economical way to transport the students is to use 10 large busses and 10 small busses.

*Note: Students may only test points (15,0), and (10, 10) due to obvious high cost of (18,2)and (18,0).

RUBRIC

Level 4: This response offers clear and convincing evidence of a deep knowledge of the mathematics related to this task.

Characteristics:
No major errors, may have minor flaws and/or omission of minor details--e.g., shading on graph may go beyond feasible region.
And
Linear system of inequalities which models the problem is correct and complete. (x,y ≥ 0 may be shown on the graph.)
And
Graph of feasible region is complete and correct.
And
Coordinate of the vertices of the feasible region are labeled on the graph or they are listed.
And
Solution of profit and the method followed is clear and correct.

Level 3: This response offers evidence of substantial knowledge of the mathematics related to this task.

Characteristics:
Linear system of inequalities which models the problem is correct and complete. ($x,y \geq 0$ may be shown on the graph.)
And
Graph of feasible region is incorrect in that a vertex is wrong.
And
Coordinate of the vertices are labeled on the graph or they are listed.
And
Solution of profit and the method followed is clear and correct--i.e., all vertices were tested (with the possible exception of (18, 0) and/or (18, 2)).
Or
Linear system of inequalities which models the problem is correct and complete. (x,y (0 may be shown on the graph.)
And
Graph of feasible region is complete and correct.
And
Coordinate of the vertices are labeled on the graph or they are listed.
And
Method of solution is incorrect in that it was assumed that the minimum cost will be found at the intersection of the two diagonal lines.

Level 2: This response offers limited or inconsistent evidence of knowledge of the mathematics related to this task.

Characteristics:
Absence of one part (A, B, or C)
Or
Two minor misconceptions or omissions in two distinct parts
Or
One major mistake or no response in one part and many minor flaws in other parts.

Level 1: This response offers little or no evidence of knowledge of the mathematics related to this task.

Characteristics:

A trial and error method is used in leading to a solution.

Or

An incorrect graph is given and there is no evidence of knowing how to use the graph to reach a solution.

Or

There is no response or the response is not germane to the task.

GET A JOB

MATHEMATICS STANDARDS ASSESSED

- Number and Operation Concepts
- Geometry and Measurement Concepts
- Function and Algebra Concepts
- Problem Solving and Mathematical Reasoning
- Mathematical Skills and Tools
- Mathematical Communication

DIRECTIONS TO THE STUDENT

Suppose you are driving on the New Jersey Turnpike to go to a new job interview in New York at 11:30 a.m. You know that you can average 55 mph on the turnpike. You must drive 50 miles to the exit you must use; it will take about 25 minutes of driving to get to the location of your appointment after you leave the turnpike. You also know that the gas tank holds 20 gallons and that you get about 18 miles per gallon on the highway.

Based on this information and the information in the picture below, do you need to stop and buy gasoline on the way to New York? If you do stop to buy gasoline, remember it will take some time to do so. Will you make it to your appointment early, on time, or late? If early or late, about how early or late would you expect to be? Explain your answers carefully.

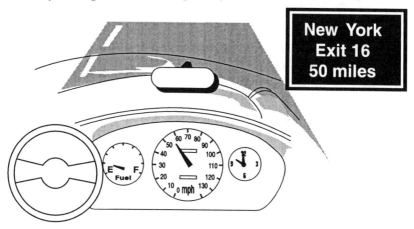

MATHEMATICAL CONCEPTS

This task provides students with the opportunity to choose and use effective problem solving strategies in dealing with this non-routine, multi-step problem. They must consider at least three time components in determining their answer. If their justification is strong, either of two answers is possible--they may be late or they may be on time.

SOLUTION

Yes, you will need to stop for gas since the fuel gauge indicates that there is 1/8 of a tank. The tank holds 20 gallons, so you have about 2.5 gallons of gas which is enough for 2.5 x 18 = 45 miles on the highway.

With respect to making the appointment on time, the following 3 basic time components should be considered:
    time to get to exit--approximately 1 hour,
    time to get gas--approximately 5 to 10 minutes, and
    time to get from exit to interview--25 minutes.
The student may also consider other components--time for parking or walking, etc.

Most responses will probably indicate that the person will be late by 5 to 20 minutes, or by a different amount is that amount is reasonably justified. However, it is possible that a student will argue that the he will be on time, and this is acceptable as long as that position is reasonably justified and the three time components listed above have been considered.

For example, a student may respond that he will probably be late by a few minutes because it is 10 am and it will take
a) about 55 min to travel 50 mi to the exit. (at 55 mph, t = [(50mi/55 mph) x 60 min/h])
b) 25 minutes to get to the exit,
c) at least 5 minutes to get gas,
and d) at least 5 minutes to walk from the car to place of the interview.
These times total at least 90 minutes which brings us to at least 11:30 am.

RUBRIC

Level 4: This response offers clear and convincing evidence of a deep knowledge of the mathematics related to this task.

Characteristics:
Student gives explicit consideration of the 3 basic time components: time to get to exit, time to get gas, and time to get from exit to interview. Student may also consider other components--time for parking or walking, etc. The response must show the computation or estimation of how far the person can travel on the remaining fuel or how much gas was needed for 50+ miles was performed reasonably. Minor computational/estimation errors may occur.

And

There is an indication that the person will not be on time by 5 to 20 minutes or by a different amount if reasonably justified. Or that person could be on time with reasonable justification. This response must be consistent with the estimations given.

Level 3: This response offers evidence of substantial knowledge of the mathematics related to this task.

Characteristics:
Student takes into account (at least implicitly) the 3 basic time components. The explanations given are not as clear as in a 4 level performance. Minor computational/estimation errors may occur.

And

The response concerning lateness (if and how much) is consistent with the estimations given.

Level 2: This response offers limited or inconsistent evidence of knowledge of the mathematics related to this task.

Characteristics:
Student makes major error in computation/estimation of, or omission of, one basic time component.

Or

Response about lateness is inconsistent with computations/estimations.

Level 1: This response offers little or no evidence of knowledge of the mathematics related to this task.

Characteristics:
Blank or irrelevant or other incorrect response is given.

IN YOUR BEST INTEREST

MATHEMATICS STANDARDS ASSESSED

- Number and Operation Concepts
- Function and Algebra Concepts
- Problem Solving and Mathematical Reasoning
- Mathematical Skills and Tools
- Mathematical Communication

DIRECTIONS TO THE STUDENT

You have earned $1,500 and want the money to grow by depositing it into a savings account at one of two banks. The *Invest With Us* bank offers an interest rate of 5.5% compounded annually. The *Make Your Money Grow* bank offers an interest rate of 5.4%. How often must the *Make Your Money Grow* bank compound your interest in order for you to make more money by investing with them? Include all possible answers, indicate your process, and explain your answer. (Please work with dollars and cents, and remember that banks round fractions of a cent down to the next penny when determining your interest.)

MATHEMATICAL CONCEPTS

In this task, students may model the problem with the function

A = P(1 + r/n)^(nt) where A= amount of money after t years assuming rollover of interest and no withdrawals, P= principal initially invested, r = rate of interest, n = number of compoundings per year, and t = number of years money is invested,

to calculate the number of compoundings that the *Make Your Money Grow* bank would have to make in one year in order to exceed the amount of money earned at the *Invest With Us Bank*. This calculation can be done by finding A for increasing values of n. The process can be carried out without or without a graphics calculator. Graphics calculators would allow the student to picture this increasing function and analyze its graph to solve the problem.

If students forget the function, $A = P(1 + r/n)^{\wedge}(nt)$, they may get the correct answer by calculating the interest at each compounding, adding it to the principal, and repeating the process until the amount of the *Make Your Money Grow* investment exceeds that of the *Invest With Us Bank* investment. This is a good exercise in recursion.

SOLUTION

At *Invest With Us*, the amount of money at the end of 1 year = $1500(1+.055/1)^{\wedge}1 = \$1582.50$. At *Make Your Money Grow*, the amount of money in your account at the end of 1 year = $1500(1+.054/n)^{\wedge}n$ which must be greater than or equal to $1582.50. This can be achieved if *Make Your Money Grow* compounds quarterly or more often. (Quarterly compounding yields $1,582.65.)

Graphics calculators may be used—tracing of the graph of $y = 1500(1+.054/x)^{\wedge}x$, evaluation of its functional values, examination of its table values, or evaluation of its intersection with the graph of $y = 1582.65$ are all viable processes. In addition, some students may forget the function which best models this situation but it is acceptable if they arrive at the correct answer by calculating the interest at each compounding, adding it to the principal, and repeating the process until the amount of the investment exceeds $1,582.50.

RUBRIC

Level 4: This response offers clear and convincing evidence of a deep knowledge of the mathematics related to this task.

Characteristics
Viable process is apparent. Calculations are correct. Correct answer is stated and explained.

Level 3: This response offers evidence of substantial knowledge of the mathematics related to this task.

Characteristics:
Viable process used, but calculations are incorrect because accuracy is not considered. That is, if student used calculations correct to the nearest hundredth, he might think that 3 compoundings are sufficient. Answer must be given and explained.

Or

Calculations are correct and lead to a statement that 4 compoundings are needed but statement does not indicate that more than 4 will also work nor is an explanation given.

Level 2: This response offers limited or inconsistent evidence of knowledge of the mathematics related to this task.

Characteristics:
Some evidence of viable process but incorrectly applies it to the data.

Or

Correctly applies to the data but never answers the question.

Or

Correctly applies to the data but makes rounding errors which lead to the wrong answer.

Or

Correctly applies to the data but appears to have arbitrarily chosen a number of compoundings which worked.

Level 1: This response offers little or no evidence of knowledge of the mathematics related to this task.

Characteristics:
Student arrives at an answer by a flawed process, such as comparing 1500 x .055 x 1 to
1500 x .054 x 2, possibly giving the correct answer with or without explanation.

EXAMPLE OF A LEVEL 4 PERFORMANCE

"Make your money flow" would have to compound 4 or more times a year for me to invest there. This is because 5.4% gives less than 5.5% annual compounding if the number of times your money is compounded is 3 or less. But after about 3.14 times the ,054 is a better deal — see the graph, it increase.

$y_1 = 1500\left(1 + \dfrac{.054}{x}\right)^x$

$y_2 = 1582.50$

$(3.14, 1582.50)$

This response is scored a 4 because:

a. The method, finding the intersection of A = 1500 $(1+.054/n)^{\wedge}n$ and A = 1582.50, is viable.

b. The stated intersection is correct.

c. The correct answer is stated and explained.

EXAMPLE OF A LEVEL 3 PERFORMANCE

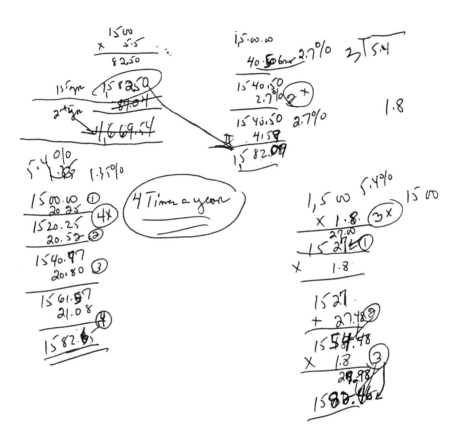

This response is scored a 3 because:
a. A viable method, repeated compounding of 5.4% until the amount of the investment exceeds $1,582.50, is apparent.
b. The method leads to a statement that 4 compoundings are needed but the statement does not indicate that more than 4 compoundings will also work nor is an explanation given.

EXAMPLE OF A LEVEL 2 PERFORMANCE

Compound 5 times) since

$$1500\left(1 + \frac{.054}{5}\right)^5 = \$1,582.77$$

This response is scored a 2 because:
There is evidence of a viable process, using A = 1500 $(1+.054/n)^n$, but it appears that 5 was arbitrarily chosen as the number of compoundings and student thought the problem was completely solved because it worked.

EXAMPLE OF LEVEL 1 PERFORMANCE

If Invest with us compounds annually the intrest accrued after 1yr will be $82.50

To do better than this "Make" must Componend at least twice a year giving $166.37 accrued the first year.

$$
\begin{array}{cccc}
1500 & 1500 & 1581 & 81 \\
\times .055 & \times .054 & \times .054 & + 85.374 \\
\hline
\$82.50 & 81 & 85.374 & 166.374 \\
\end{array}
$$

This response is scored a 1 because the student arrived at an answer using a flawed process.

LET'S GET PHYSICAL

MATHEMATICS STANDARDS ASSESSED

- Number and Operation Concepts
- Function and Algebra Concepts
- Statistics and Probability Concepts
- Problem Solving and Mathematical Reasoning
- Mathematical Skills and Tools
- Mathematical Communication

DIRECTIONS TO THE STUDENT

The results of a questionnaire filled out by a student body of one thousand students determined that their most frequent methods of exercise were running, lifting, and skating. The results showed that

260 students ran.
360 students lifted.
240 students skated.
100 students ran and lifted.
80 students ran and skated.
120 students lifted and skated.
60 students ran, lifted, and skated.

1. Construct a Venn Diagram and record the number of students in each region.

2. a. How many students only lift to exercise?
   b. How many students run or lift to exercise?
   c. How many students run and lift, but do not skate to exercise?
   d. How many students do not run, lift, or skate?

3. If you were in charge of scheduling exercise availability and could only schedule 2 activities for any time slot, which two of the three most popular exercises would you schedule most frequently? Explain and justify your answer.

MATHEMATICAL CONCEPTS

To solve this task, students must organize and analyze the intersections and unions of the data via a Venn Diagram. They must then solve an authentic problem based on that analysis.

SOLUTION

1. Venn Diagram:

Student Body

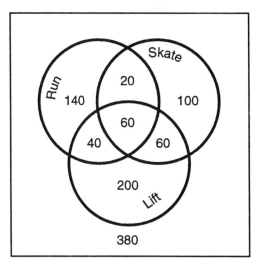

2. a. $200 = 360 - (60 + 60 + 40)$
   b. $520 = 260 + 260$
   c. $40 = 100 - 60$
   d. $380 = 1000 - (140 + 40 + 60 + 20 + 200 + 60 + 100)$

3. More than one answer is acceptable but the reasoning must be sound in order for an answer to be accepted. For example, a student may say that running and skating should be scheduled most often for the same time slot since this would minimize conflicts--120 both lift and skate, 100 students both run and lift, but only 80 students run and skate. Or, a student might respond that lifting and running should be scheduled in the same time slot since this would attract 420 (=200+ 60 +140 +20) people without conflict, whereas lifting and skating would attract 360 (=200 + 40 +100 + 20) people without conflict, and running and skating would attract only 340 (=140 + 40 + 100 + 60) people without conflict.

RUBRIC

Level 4: This response offers clear and convincing evidence of a deep knowledge of the mathematics related to this task.

Characteristics:
All parts correct with the possibility of a minor flaw. Part 3 must show correct reasoning. (It is possible to score a 4 if an error was made in the Venn Diagram but the answers and reasoning given in parts 2 and 3 are correct based on that error.)

Level 3: This response offers evidence of substantial knowledge of the mathematics related to this task.

Characteristics:
Multiple minor flaws in parts 1 and 2 but reasoning correct in part 3.

Level 2: This response offers limited or inconsistent evidence of knowledge of the mathematics related to this task.

Characteristics:
Parts 1& 2 correct, but part 3 weak, incorrect, or missing.
Or
Major flaws in part 1 and/or 2, but reasoning correct in part 3.

Level 1:   This response offers little or no evidence of knowledge of the mathematics related to this task.

Characteristics:
Major flaws in Parts 1 and 2 and part 3 weak or missing.

Matrices in Manufacturing

Mathematics Standards Assessed

- Number and Operation Concepts
- Function and Algebra Concepts
- Problem Solving and Mathematical Reasoning
- Mathematical Skills and Tools

Directions to the Student

A computer manufacturer has three factories at which their products are made. Number of units sold last year (in thousands) are stated in the matrix below.

$$
\begin{array}{c}
\\
\text{Laptop} \\
\text{Desk Top} \\
\text{Printer} \\
\text{Scanner}
\end{array}
\begin{array}{ccc}
\text{Factory A} & \text{Factory B} & \text{Factory C} \\
\left[\begin{array}{ccc}
5 & 4 & 6 \\
10 & 12 & 11 \\
8 & 10 & 10 \\
3 & 2.5 & 2.1
\end{array}\right] & & = N
\end{array}
$$

a. The selling price of a laptop is \$2200, a desk top is \$2600, a printer is \$450, and a scanner is \$730. Show this information in a matrix P.

b. Use matrices N and P to find matrix R which gives the total revenue (in thousands) at each factory. Be sure that your process is evident, that each matrix is written out, and that R is identified.

c. With respect to matrix R and this problem, what information is given by the value a_{12}?

d. In dollars, what was this company's total revenue last year?

MATHEMATICAL CONCEPTS

In this task, students see matrices as a way of storing and easily manipulating data in an authentic setting. Use of a graphics calculator further enhances their appreciation of the power of matrices. Students, with or without calculator, must consider matrix dimension, positional significance of matrix elements, and interpret a matrix product in order to solve this task.

SOLUTION

a. P = [2200 2600 450 730]. Note: A 4x1 matrix could be used to represent this data. However, this dimension will not allow for multiplication by matrix N.

b. $P \times N = R$

$$[2200\ 2600\ 450\ 730] \times \begin{bmatrix} 5 & 4 & 6 \\ 10 & 12 & 11 \\ 81 & 0 & 10 \\ 3 & 2..5 & 2.1 \end{bmatrix} = [42{,}790\ 46{,}325\ 47{,}833]$$

c. a_{12} represents factory B's revenue last year.

d. 42,790,000 + 46,325,000 + 47,833,000 = $136,948,000

RUBRIC

Level 4: This response offers clear and convincing evidence of a deep knowledge of the mathematics related to this task.

Characteristics:
Matrices are shown, correct process is evident, and computations are correct.
Or
Matrices are shown, correct process is evident, and computations are correct with minor errors--e.g., transcribing a matrix element incorrectly.

Level 3: This response offers evidence of substantial knowledge of the mathematics related to this task.

Characteristics:
An arithmetical error is made in multiplication of matrices but it is apparent that the student has put row on column throughout the multiplication.

Or

Student's methodology is correct throughout, but answers are incorrect due to arithmetical error only.

Or

Parts a, b, and d are correct, but c is incorrect.

Level 2: This response offers limited or inconsistent evidence of knowledge of the mathematics related to this task.

Characteristics:
Parts a and b are correct, but c and d are incorrect.

Level 1: This response offers little or no evidence of knowledge of the mathematics related to this task.

Characteristics:
Part b is incorrect due to lack of understanding of matrix multiplication.

Or

Part b is correct but it is not apparent that matrices were used to find the answers to part b.

MEAN SALARIES

MATHEMATICS STANDARDS ASSESSED

- Number and Operation Concepts
- Function and Algebra Concepts
- Statistics and Probability Concepts
- Problem Solving and Mathematical Reasoning
- Mathematical Skills and Tools
- Mathematical Communication

DIRECTIONS TO THE STUDENT

The annual salaries of all the employees of a small company are listed below.

President: $110,000
Vice President: $60,000
Senior Professionals $50,000; $48,000; $48,000; $44,000
Junior Professionals: $36,000; $36,000; $36,000; $32,000
Clerical Staff: $22,000; $18,000; $14,000

a. What are the mean, the median, and the mode of the salaries of the employees of this company?
b. How is each of these statistics affected if the President's salary is excluded?
c. What do your findings tell you about the statistic that should probably be used in discussions of the salary of a typical professional baseball player? Explain.

MATHEMATICAL CONCEPTS

This task gives students the opportunity to see the effect of an outlier on statistics. In addition, they must think analytically about the differences between the mean, median, and mode in representing data.

SOLUTIONS

a.   Mean is $42,615.38 (or close to this amount), median is $36,000, and mode is $36,000.

b. If the president's salary is eliminated, the median and mode will be unaffected but the mean would decrease.

c. The median or mode would be more realistic than the mean for discussion of salaries. This is because the mean would be forced upward by the huge salaries of superstars.

RUBRIC

Level 4: This response offers clear and convincing evidence of a deep knowledge of the mathematics related to this task.

Characteristics:
Correct median and mode and correct process and reasonable value for mean--error due to omission of data or minor computational error is acceptable;

And

Correct effect on each statistic if President's salary is eliminated;

And

Indication that median or mode is better than the mean for discussion of salaries with reasonable explanation.

Level 3:   This response offers evidence of substantial knowledge of the mathematics related to this task.

Characteristics:
Two of the level 4 requirements are satisfactorily met and one is missing or unsatisfactory;

Or

One requirement is satisfactorily met and others are partially satisfactory.

Level 2: This response offers limited or inconsistent evidence of knowledge of the mathematics related to this task.

Characteristics:
One of the level 4 requirements is satisfactorily met, and others are missing or unsatisfactory;
Or
Two or three requirements are partially satisfactory.

Level 1: This response offers little or no evidence of knowledge of the mathematics related to this task.

Characteristics:
Unsatisfactory with respect to all three level 4 requirements;
Or
Blank, or irrelevant or other incorrect responses.

A PAINTER'S SOLUTION

MATHEMATICS STANDARDS ASSESSED

- Number and Operation Concepts
- Geometry and Measurement Concepts
- Function and Algebra Concepts
- Problem Solving and Mathematical Reasoning
- Mathematical Skills and Tools
- Mathematical Communication

DIRECTIONS TO THE STUDENT

Raphael visited the White House and was awed by the beauty of the Blue Room. He was so awed, that he is going to paint his living room the very same shade of blue. Since he is a very busy person, he plans to spread the work out so that he can do some painting each day until the job is done. He will start with the largest wall and paint half of it today. Tomorrow, he will paint half of what remains to be painted on that wall. And he will continue in this fashion, each day painting half of the unpainted part of the wall, until he completely paints the wall. When can he start painting the next wall? Provide a diagram and a mathematical justification for your answer.

MATHEMATICAL CONCEPTS

In order to solve this problem, students will either formally or informally model the amount of the wall that is painted as a geometric series. Zeno's Paradox comes into play when they realize that theoretically the series will not equal 1 whole wall until an infinite number of days have passed.

SOLUTION

The amount of painting completed at the end of day n is modeled by the geometric series: $1/2 + 1/4 + 1/8 + ... + 1/2^n$. The sum of which equals $a[(1-r^n)/(1-r)]$ or in this case,

$(1/2)[1 - ((1/2)^n)]/(1-1/2) = 1- (1/2)^n$. As n increases, $1 - (1/2)^n$ approaches 1, but will not equal 1 unless n = infinity. Application of the formula $a/(1-r)$ will give the sum of 1 and may be used to arrive at an answer. Therefore, a student's answer may be no, if the student answers theoretically, since Raphael cannot paint for an infinite number of days. Or they may answer yes since after a few days the amount of the wall that is unpainted will be too small to subdivide and one brush stroke will finish the job. The student should address the paradox between the theoretical and practical. The diagram should illustrate the geometric progression.

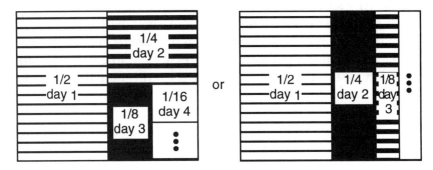

RUBRIC

Level 4: This response offers clear and convincing evidence of a deep knowledge of the mathematics related to this task.

Characteristics:
Diagram reflects geometric progression. Mathematical justification is rigorous with indication that paradox exists--i.e., series never sums to one but wall gets painted.

Level 3: This response offers evidence of substantial knowledge of the mathematics related to this task.

Characteristics:
Diagram reflects geometric progression. Mathematical justification is rigorous but there is no indication that a paradox exists.

Or

Diagram reflects geometric progression. Mathematical justification is good but not rigorous with indication that paradox exists.

Or

Diagram is missing but mathematical justification is rigorous with indication that paradox exists.

Level 2: This response offers limited or inconsistent evidence of knowledge of the mathematics related to this task.

Characteristics:

This response offers limited or inconsistent evidence of knowledge of the mathematics related to this task. Characteristics: Diagram reflects geometric progression. Mathematical justification is intuitive with little or no indication that paradox exists.

Level 1: This response offers little or no evidence of knowledge of the mathematics related to this task.

Characteristics:

Offers no mathematical justification or mathematical justification is erroneous.
Diagram may be present.

EXAMPLE OF A LEVEL 4 PERFORMANCE

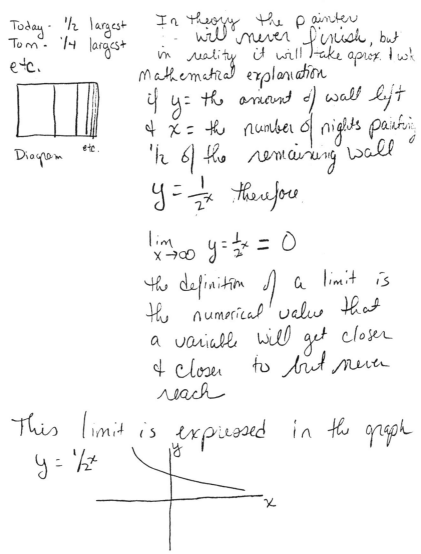

Today - $\frac{1}{2}$ largest
Tom - $\frac{1}{4}$ largest
etc.

Diagram　etc.

In theory the painter will never finish, but in reality it will take aprox. 1 wk

Mathematical explanation

if y = the amount of wall left & x = the number of nights painting $\frac{1}{2}$ of the remaining wall

$y = \frac{1}{2^x}$ therefore

$\lim\limits_{x \to \infty} y = \frac{1}{2^x} = 0$

the definition of a limit is the numerical value that a variable will get closer & closer to but never reach

This limit is expressed in the graph $y = \frac{1}{2^x}$

This response is scored a 4 because the diagram reflects the geometric progression, the mathematical justification is rigorous, and because the student has clearly indicated that a paradox exists.

EXAMPLE OF A LEVEL 3 PERFORMANCE

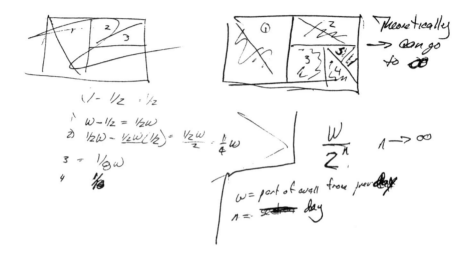

This response is scored a 3 because the diagram reflects the geometric progression, the mathematical justification is good but not rigorous, and because the word "theoretical" is used the student has indicated that a paradox exists.

EXAMPLE OF A LEVEL 2 PERFORMANCE

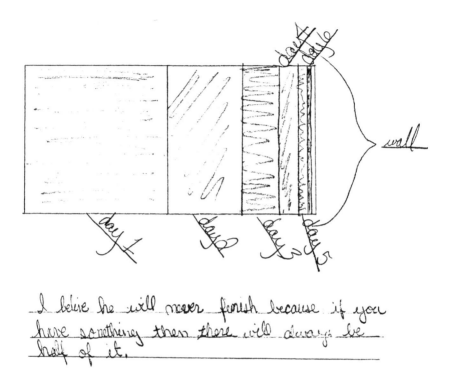

I belive he will never finish because if you have something then there will always be half of it.

This response is scored a 2 because the diagram reflects the geometric progression, the mathematical justification is intuitive, and because the student has not indicated that a paradox exists.

EXAMPLE OF A LEVEL 1 PERFORMANCE

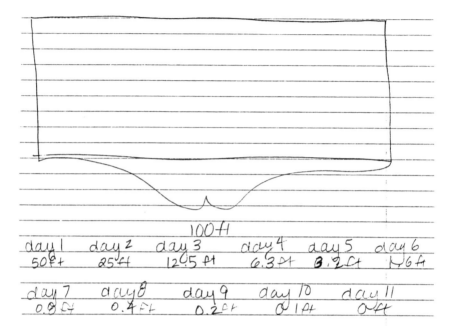

100 ft

day 1	day 2	day 3	day 4	day 5	day 6
50 ft	25 ft	12.5 ft	6.3 ft	3.2 ft	1.6 ft

day 7	day 8	day 9	day 10	day 11
0.8 ft	0.4 ft	0.2 ft	0.1 ft	0 ft

This response is scored a 1 because their mathematical justification is erroneous.

PENNY WISE

MATHEMATICS STANDARDS ASSESSED

- Number and Operation Concepts
- Geometry and Measurement Concepts
- Function and Algebra Concepts
- Mathematical Skills and Tools
- Problem Solving and Mathematical Reasoning
- Mathematical Communication

DIRECTIONS TO THE STUDENT

The Sears Tower in Chicago, Illinois is the tallest building in the United States. It was built in 1974 and measures 1,454 feet in height from sidewalk to roof. Suppose that a penny is to be dropped off the roof of the tower. Assume negligible air resistance, show how you arrived at your answer indicating the units throughout, and round to the nearest tenth when you answer the following questions.

a. How high is the penny 3 seconds after it is dropped?
b. How long does it take the penny to hit the sidewalk?
c. What is the velocity of the penny when it hits the sidewalk?
d. What is the speed of the penny, in miles per hour, when it hits the sidewalk?
e. What do you think happens when the penny hits the sidewalk?

MATHEMATICAL CONCEPT

Solution of this problem requires application of the height and velocity functions for rectilinear motion within a vacuum. Because the Sears Tower does not exist within a vacuum, students should discuss the limitation of these mathematical models. Calculus students should be given only the height function, so that they can derive the velocity function. In addition, students should understand that speed is the absolute value of velocity.

The height function is $h(t) = .5g(t^2) + v(0) t + h(0)$ where $h(t)$ is the height of the projectile t seconds after it is projected; $g = -32$ ft/sec^2 is the acceleration of gravity ; $v(0)$ is the initial velocity of the projectile in ft/sec^2; and $h(0)$ is the initial height of the projectile in feet.

The velocity function is $v(t) = g t + v(0)$, where $v(t)$ is the velocity of the projectile t seconds after it is projected; $g = -32$ ft/sec^2 is the acceleration of gravity; and $v(0)$ is the initial velocity of the projectile in ft/sec^2.

Units are requested throughout to give students experience in dimensional analysis. Too often, units are not considered by students until they state the final answer.

Part e of the prompt can be used to segue into an investigation of the physics of collision.

SOLUTION

a. $h(3) = .5$ (-32 ft/sec^2)[(3 sec)^2] + (0 ft/sec)(3 sec) + 1454 ft
  $= 1310$ ft

b. $h(t) = 0$ ft $= .5$(-32 ft/sec^2)[(t sec)^2] + 0(3 sec) + 1,454 ft
  0 ft $= -16$ t^2 ft + 1454 ft
  16 t^2 $= 1454$
  ≈ 9.5 sec

c. $v(9.5) = -32$ ft/sec^2)(9.5 sec) + 0 ft/sec^2
  $= -304$ ft /sec

d. (304 ft/sec) (1 mile/5280 ft) (3600 sec/hr) ≈ 207.3 mph

e. Answers will vary, but it is probable that, due to the speed at which the penny is traveling when it hits the ground, most students will indicate that the penny will damage the sidewalk and/or bounce.

RUBRIC

(Caution: Although an answer is expected, question e is meant to stimulate discussion rather than count heavily toward scoring.)

Level 4: This response offers clear and convincing evidence of a deep knowledge of the mathematics related to this task.

Characteristics:
Functions are used properly, with correct units shown throughout, answers are correct. The answer to part e is reasonable. Minor errors may occur--e.g., speed is stated as a negative.

Or

Functions are used properly, answers are correct, but units are missing in one part of the problem. The answer to part e is reasonable.

Or

Functions are used properly, with correct units shown throughout, answers are correct but are not rounded to the nearest tenth. The answer to part e is reasonable.

Level 3: This response offers evidence of substantial knowledge of the mathematics related to this task.

Characteristics:
Any of the above but part e is not answered.

Or

One of the answers a-d is incorrect because of an error in calculation--e.g., the height or velocity function is correctly selected but incorrectly transcribed, or a value is incorrectly substituted for a variable. All others show correct answers and use of functions. The answer to part e is reasonable.

Level 2: This response offers limited or inconsistent evidence of knowledge of the mathematics related to this task.

Characteristics:
One of the answers a-d is incorrect because of incorrect use of

a function. Minor errors may also occur--e.g., units are forgotten. All else is correct. Part e may be weak or missing.

Or

Two of answers a-d are incorrect because of error in calculation--e.g., the height or velocity function is correctly selected but incorrectly transcribed, or a value is incorrectly substituted for a variable. All else is correct except that part e may be missing. Units may be missing.

Level 1: This response offers little or no evidence of knowledge of the mathematics related to this task.

Characteristics:

Only one of the answers correct with the correct work. Part e may be missing.

Or

Student uses correct functions but incorrectly uses variables throughout--e.g., time is confused with height. As a result, although work is shown for a-d, all answers are incorrect. Part e may be missing.

Or

Answers appear but no work is shown.

Or

Incorrect functions are used throughout. There is little evidence of understanding the concepts involved. The answer to part e may or may not be reasonable.

EXAMPLE OF A LEVEL 4 PERFORMANCE

a. $h(3) = \frac{1}{2}(-32)(3^2) + 0 \cdot 3 + 1454 = 1310$

b. $h(t) = 0 = -16 \, t^2 + 1454$

$16 \, t^2 = 1454$

$t^2 = 90.875$

$t = 9.5 \, sec$

c. $V(9.5) = -32 \cdot 9.5 = -304 \frac{ft}{sec}$

d. $S = -304 \cdot 60 \cdot 60 \div 5280 = -207.3 \, mph$

e. Might dent sidewalk – it's moving fast!
will also bounce off sidewalk – I think

This student received a score of 4 because functions were used properly, answers are correct except for minor errors--units were not given in part 1 and speed was expressed as a negative. The answer to part e is reasonable.

EXAMPLE OF A LEVEL 3 PERFORMANCE

A) $h(t) = .5g(t^2) + V_o t + h_o$

$h(3) = .5 \cdot -32(9) + 0(3) + 1454$

$h(3) = -144 + 1454$

$h(3) = 1310$

$h = 1310 ft$

B) $0(t) = .5 \cdot -32(t^2) + 0(t) + 1454$

$= 1454 = -16 t^2$

$\dfrac{-16}{} \quad \dfrac{-16}{}$

$t = \sqrt{90.875} \doteq 9.5 \, sec$

C) $v(t) = gt + V_o$

$v(9.5) = -32(9.5) + 0$

$v(9.5) = -304$

$v = 3.47$

D) See above

E) It bounces up.

This response is scored a 3 because functions were used properly, answers are correct except that part d was not done--student assumed speed was the same as velocity and student appears to have missed the mph requirement. The answer to part e is reasonable.

EXAMPLE OF A LEVEL 2 PERFORMANCE

a) $h = -16(9) + 0(9) + 0$

$= -144\ ft$

$h = 1454 - 144$

$= 1310\ ft$

b) $-1454 = -16\ t^{-2} + 1454$

$16\ t^2 = 2908$

$t^2 = 181.75$

$t = \overline{13.47} \quad 13.\ 48\ sec$

c) $V = -32 \cdot 13.48 + 0$

$-431.8\ ft/sec$

d) $\dfrac{-431.4\ ft}{sec} \cdot \dfrac{3600\ sec}{hr} \cdot \dfrac{1\ mi}{5280\ ft}$

$= 294.1\ mph$

e) something

This response is scored a 2 because the answer to b is incorrect due to the misinterpretation of h(t). The answers to c and d are acceptable based on the answer to b. However, the answer to part e is weak. (Note: this would have been a 3 paper had the answer to part e been strong.)

EXAMPLE OF A LEVEL 1 PERFORMANCE

a) $v_f = v_0 + at$

$V_f = 0 + (9.8 \text{ }^m/_{s^2})(3s)$

$V_f = 29.4 \text{ }^m/s$

b) $d = v_0 t + \frac{1}{2}at^2$

$1454 = 0 + \frac{1}{2}(9.8)t^2$

$1454 = \frac{1}{2}(9.8)(t)^2$

$296.7 = t^2$

$17.2 = t$

c) $V_f = V_0 + at$

$V_f = 0 + (9.8 \text{ }^m/_{s^2})(17.2s)$

$V_f = 168.56 \text{ }^m/s$

d) $\dfrac{168.56 \text{ m}}{s} \Big| \dfrac{3600s}{1hr} \Big| \dfrac{100 \text{ cm}}{1m} \Big| \dfrac{1 in}{2.5 cm} \Big| \dfrac{ft}{12 in} \Big| \dfrac{1 mi}{5280 ft} \Big| = 377.05 \text{ }^{mi}/_{1}$

e) most of the energy is spent on the side walk possibl cracking it, some of the energy is returned to the penny causing it to bounce.   PWE

This response is scored a 1 because incorrect functions are used throughout. There is little evidence of understanding of the concepts involved. The answer to e is quite good.

Pool Construction

Mathematics Standards Assessed

- Number and Operation Concepts
- Geometry and Measurement Concepts
- Function and Algebra Concepts
- Problem Solving and Mathematical Reasoning
- Mathematical Skills and Tools
- Mathematical Communication

Directions to the Student

Suppose that a community is thinking of hiring your company to increase the size of their swimming pool. The dimensions of the existing pool are given below. The community has undergone considerable growth and they would like to increase pool memberships by 25%. In addition, they want to maintain the current hours of operation and make the pool available to all members during those times. Write a proposal for presentation to the mayor and council. Be sure that your proposal:

    a. includes a labeled diagram,

    b. explains why the new pool will accommodate 25% more members,

    c. gives the surface area of the new pool as compared to that of the present pool,

    d. gives the amount of water needed to fill the new pool as compared to that needed to fill the existing pool, and

    e. indicates all units of measure.

The surface area of the water in the pool is a 24′ by 48′ rectangle. The side view of the pool is uniform and shows its dimensions.

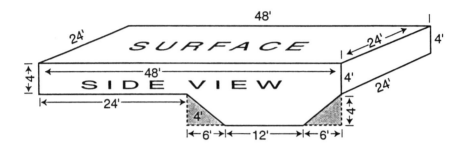

MATHEMATICAL CONCEPT

To complete this task, students must be able to find the volume of an irregular solid, and they must find a way to increase that volume by increasing the surface area of the water, so that pool membership may be increased by 25 %. In addition, they must be able to communicate their plan in order to convince others of its merit.

SOLUTION

Many solutions are possible but those which are viable must increase the surface area of the water in the pool by 25%. One way to accomplish this is to increase the length or width of that surface by 25%. For instance, students may increase the width to 30 ft and leave the length unchanged, or they may increase the length to 60 ft and leave the width unchanged. Another way to accomplish the change is to both dimensions. For instance, they could increase the width by a factor of 3 and the reduce the length by a factor of 5/12, yielding a 72′ x 20′ surface area. In any case, the surface area should increase from 1,152 sq ft to 1440 sq ft.

In order to calculate the volume of the existing pool, students should find the cross-sectional side area by breaking it up into a 4 x 48 rectangle, and a trapezoid with bases of 24 and 12 and height of 4. These areas, respectively 192 and 72, sum to 264 sq ft. This cross-sectional area of 264 sq ft should be multiplied by 24 ft, the width of the pool, yielding a volume of 6,336 cubic feet. That is, V = [48 x 4 + 4(12 + 24)/2] x 24 =6,336. If length does not change, then the new volume will be 1.25 of the old volume or 7,920 cu ft. However if the length changes, other volumes are possible and must be considered on their merit.

Note: Increasing the volume of the pool by increasing a dimension other than length or width of the surface area of the water, simply increases the depth of the pool. It will not allow for increased membership.

RUBRIC

Level 4: This response offers clear and convincing evidence of a deep knowledge of the mathematics related to this task.

Characteristics
The diagram is 3 dimensional and correctly labeled.
The surface area is correctly calculated, and compared to the original area.
The volume of water is correct and compared to the original volume.
The solution to the problem is viable and the explanation is correct.

Level 3: This response offers evidence of substantial knowledge of the mathematics related to this task.

Characteristics:
The diagram shows only the surface of the pool but is correctly labeled.
The surface area and volume of the water are correctly calculated but may not be compared to the original amounts.

The solution to the problem is viable and the explanation can be followed but is incomplete probably due to the lack of comparisons to the original conditions.

Level 2: This response offers limited or inconsistent evidence of knowledge of the mathematics related to this task.

Characteristics:
The diagram is incomplete or not labeled.
The surface area is given without comparison to original area.
The volume of water is given without comparison to the original volume.
The solution to the problem is viable but the explanation is missing or incomprehensible.

Level 1: This response offers little or no evidence of knowledge of the mathematics related to this task.

Characteristics:
The diagram has the wrong shape or is missing.
The surface area is incorrectly calculated or missing.
The volume of water is incorrectly calculated or missing.
The solution to the problem is missing or not feasible.

PRICE RESTORATION

MATHEMATICS STANDARDS ASSESSED

- Number and Operation Concepts
- Problem Solving and Mathematical Reasoning
- Mathematical Skills and Tools
- Mathematical Communication

DIRECTIONS TO THE STUDENT

For a sale, a shopkeeper lowered the original price of an item by 30 percent. After the sale, the shop keeper told his clerk, Mike, to raise the price of that item by 30 percent of its sale price. So, Mike marked the item with its original price. Was Mike right or wrong in doing that? Present a convincing argument to support your answer; you may wish to include a simple, specific example as part of your argument.

MATHEMATICAL CONCEPTS

This prompt requires that students think about percent in a critical way. They will see percent as an amount which varies with the base, unlike a constant amount.

SOLUTIONS

Mike was wrong. 30% of the original price does not equal 30% of the sale price because the sale price is less than the original price. They can illustrate this abstractly or with a specific example:

Abstractly, let x = the original price, then $.7x$ is the sale price, and 30% of the sale price is $.21x$. If Mike had followed the manager's direction, he should have added $.21x$ to $.7x$, getting $.91x$ rather than x.

For example, if the original price were $100, the sale price would be $70, and 30% of the reduced price would be $21. If Mike had followed the manager's direction, he should have added $21 to $70 , getting $91 rather than the original price of $100.

RUBRIC

Level 4: This response offers clear and convincing evidence of a deep knowledge of the mathematics related to this task.

Characteristics:
Student indicates that the clerk was wrong and presents a complete and convincing argument.

Level 3: This response offers evidence of substantial knowledge of the mathematics related to this task.

Characteristics:
Student indicates that the clerk was wrong and presents a complete and convincing argument but there are minor computational errors.

Level 2: This response offers limited or inconsistent evidence of knowledge of the mathematics related to this task.

Characteristics:
Student indicates that the clerk was wrong but presents a weak or incomplete argument.
Or
Student indicates that the clerk was wrong and presents a clear argument but the computations are wrong.

Level 1: This response offers little or no evidence of knowledge of the mathematics related to this task.

Characteristics:
Student gives an inappropriate answer or no answer.

A RECTANGULAR PLOT

MATHEMATICS STANDARDS ASSESSED

- Number and Operation Concepts
- Geometry and Measurement Concepts
- Function and Algebra Concepts
- Problem Solving and Mathematical Reasoning
- Mathematical Skills and Tools
- Mathematical Communication

DIRECTIONS TO THE STUDENT

Suppose that you want to enclose a 650 sq m rectangular plot of land along a river. What can the dimensions of the plot be if you have only 110 m of fencing and you do not fence the river side? Provide a labeled diagram and show the method you used to arrive at your answer. If a graphing utility is used, indicate how it was used, and if applicable, sketch and label curves and any significant points. (Round answers to the nearest tenth.)

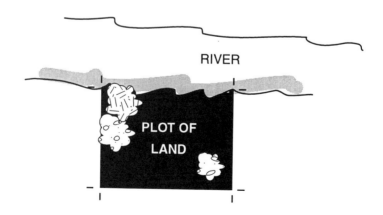

MATHEMATICAL CONCEPTS

In order to complete this task, most students will probably model the problem with a system of equations and then decide which method they will use to solve the system. They should realize that there are 2 sets of dimensions that will satisfy the given conditions. Those students who try to complete the task by using the *Solve* function on their calculators will soon realize the limits of technology.

SOLUTIONS

Method 1: Graph L vs W, and find the intersection of the line and the hyperbola. Since L and W are positive, we need only look at the branch of the hyperbola in the first quadrant. Note: Axes may be interchanged.

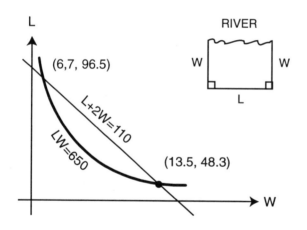

System is:
L + 2W = 110 or y = 110 - 2x
LW = 650   or y = 650 / x

Dimensions are:
48.3m x 13.5m
or
6.7m   x 96.5m

Method 2: Using substitution, get an equation in W which models the problem:

$W^2 - 55W + 325 = 0$. Then find the roots of this equation to find the widths.

Use these widths to find the lengths.

(Note: Students may prefer to model the problem in terms of L:

$$L^2 - 110L + 1300 = 0)$$

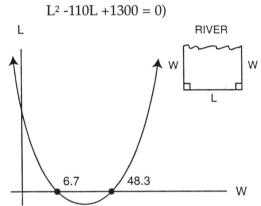

$LW = 650$
$(110-2W)W = 650$
$2W^2 - 110W + 650 = 0$
$W^2 - 55W + 325 = 0$

Dimensions are:
48.3m x 13.5m
or
6.7m x 96.5m

Method 3: Use substitution and the quadratic formula to find the solutions for one dimension, and then solve for the other dimension.

Method 4: Guess and check, possibly making a table and exploring possibilities, to arrive at the solutions.

Note: The solve function on graphics calculators will give only one solution.

RUBRIC

Level 4: This response offers clear and convincing evidence of a deep knowledge of the mathematics related to this task.

Characteristics:
Student correctly solves the problem by one of the methods given. Both solutions are given. Work may have minor flaws--e.g., intersection not labeled, or one of the answers may not be correctly rounded.

Level 3: This response offers evidence of substantial knowledge of the mathematics related to this task.

Characteristics:
Student attempts to solve the problem by one of the given methods and both solutions are correct except for one incorrect or omitted dimension.

Level 2: This response offers limited or inconsistent evidence of knowledge of the mathematics related to this task.

Characteristics:
Student attempts to solve the problem by one of the methods given but states only one set of correct dimensions; or states only the widths and not the lengths of both sets of dimensions or vice versa; or the student states both lengths or both widths as one set of dimensions.

Level 1: This response offers little or no evidence of knowledge of the mathematics related to this task.

Characteristics:
Student attempts to solve the problem by one of the methods given but cannot correctly state any part of either set of dimensions, or only one dimension of one set is correct.

EXAMPLE OF A LEVEL 4 PERFORMANCE

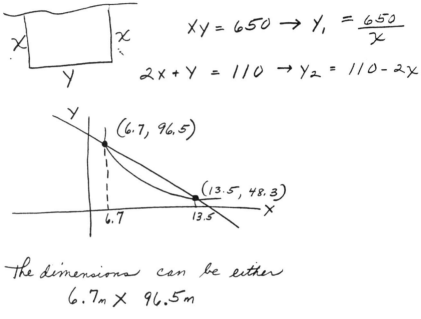

$$xy = 650 \rightarrow y_1 = \frac{650}{x}$$

$$2x + y = 110 \rightarrow y_2 = 110 - 2x$$

The dimensions can be either

6.7m × 96.5m

or

13.5m × 48.3m

This response is scored a 4 because student correctly solved the problem by an acceptable methods. Both solutions are given. Work does have a minor flaws--curves are not labeled.

EXAMPLE OF A LEVEL 3 PERFORMANCE

$y \boxed{\overset{x}{650}} y$

$x \cdot y = 650$

$x + 2y = 110$

$x = \dfrac{650}{y}$

$\dfrac{650}{y} + 2y = 110$

$\dfrac{650 + 2y^2}{y} = 110$

$650 + 2y^2 = 110y$

$2y^2 - 110y + 650 = 0$

$x = 13.5$
$y = 48.3$

$y = \dfrac{-b \pm \sqrt{b^2 - 4ac}}{2a}$

$y = \dfrac{-(-110) \pm \sqrt{(-110)^2 - 4(2)(650)}}{2(2)}$

$y = \dfrac{110 \pm \sqrt{12100 - 5200}}{4}$

$y = \dfrac{110 \pm \sqrt{6900}}{4}$

$y = \dfrac{110 \pm 83.1}{4}$

$y = 13.5 \; ; \; 48.3$

$x = 48.1 \qquad 13.5$

This response is scored a 3 because the student solved the problem by an acceptable method and realized that there are two sets of dimensions. However, in solving by the quadratic formula, an error was made in one value of the width (13.5) and this resulted in an incorrect set of dimensions: 13.5 x 48.1.

EXAMPLE OF A LEVEL 2 PERFORMANCE

$$l + 2w = 110$$
$$lw = 650$$
$$(110 - 2w)\,w = 650$$
$$110w - 2w^2 = 650$$
$$2w^2 - 110w + 650 = 0$$
$$y = 2x^2 - 110x + 650$$

Dimensions: 6.7 × 48.3

This response is scored a 2 because the student attempts to solve the problem by one of the methods given but misinterprets the function graphed and states both widths as one set of dimensions.

EXAMPLE OF A LEVEL 1 PERFORMANCE

$x \cdot y = 650$

$650 m^2$

$x + y = 110$

$x = \dfrac{650}{y}$

$\dfrac{650}{y} + y = 110$

$\dfrac{650 + y^2}{y} = 110$

$650 + y^2 = 110y$

$y^2 - 110y + 650 = 0$

$x = \dfrac{-b \pm \sqrt{b^2 - 4ac}}{2a}$

$y = \dfrac{-(-110) \pm \sqrt{110^2 - 4(1)(650)}}{2(1)}$

$y = \dfrac{110 \pm \sqrt{12100 - 2600}}{2}$

$y = \dfrac{110 \pm \sqrt{9500}}{2}$

$y = \dfrac{110 \pm 97.46}{2}$

$y = 6.25 \ \& \ 103.8$

This response is scored a 1 because the student attempted to solve the problem by one of the methods given but did not correctly state any part of either set of dimensions. Specifically, the student did not model the perimeter condition correctly--had the diagram been labeled this error may have been avoided. In addition, though the quadratic formula was applied correctly, the answers were interpreted as one set of dimensions.

SEE THE LIGHT

MATHEMATICS STANDARDS ASSESSED

- Number and Operation Concepts
- Geometry and Measurement Concepts
- Function and Algebra Concepts
- Problem Solving and Mathematical Reasoning
- Mathematical Communication Mathematical Communication

DIRECTIONS TO THE STUDENT

An artisan has been hired to repair a leaded glass window which looks as pictured below. The glass is held in the window by its wooden frame and by six diagonal lead strips. If the artisan must replace all six diagonal strips and the lead is sold in centimeter lengths only, what is the total length of lead she must provide? Round your final answer to the nearest whole centimeter which will allow for enough lead to complete the job and indicate the processes you used to get your answer.

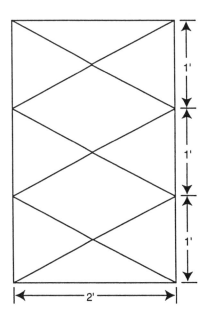

MATHEMATICAL CONCEPTS

In this task, students must apply the concept of congruence and the Pythagorean relationship. They will recognize that the diagonal strips are all congruent and that they are also hypotenuses. Dimensional analysis is also required since students must convert inches to centimeters.

SOLUTION

All six diagonal strips are congruent, and those which attach to the corners of the window are hypotenuses of the right triangles in the diagram. Thus, the problem may be solved by recognizing that relationship and applying the Pythagorean Theorem:

$c^2 = 1^2 + 2^2$, $c = \sqrt{5}$; therefore, the amount of lead required is
$6 \sqrt{5} \text{ feet} = (6\sqrt{5} \text{ feet}) \times (12 \text{ inches}/1 \text{ feet}) \times (2.54 \text{ cm}/1 \text{ inch}) \approx 409 \text{ cm}.$

It is also possible that the student will recognize that the altitude to the base of the isosceles triangle at the bottom of the window is .5 inches, use the Pythagorean Theorem to solve for a half of a diagonal, and then multiple by 12 to get the answer:

$c^2 = 1^2 + .5^2 = 1.25$, $c = \sqrt{1.25}$; therefore, the amount of lead required is
$(12\sqrt{1.25} \text{ feet}) \times (12 \text{ inches}/1 \text{ feet}) \times (2.54 \text{ cm}/1 \text{ inch}) \approx 409 \text{ cm}.$

RUBRIC

Level 4: This response offers clear and convincing evidence of a deep knowledge of the mathematics related to this task.

Characteristics:
The process is correct as are the calculations along the way. The final answer must be 409 cm.

Level 3: This response offers evidence of substantial knowledge of the mathematics related to this task.

Characteristics:
The student is able to get the answer in feet but seriously errs in dimensional analysis.

Or

The student applies the Pythagorean and congruence concepts correctly, and knows how to convert to centimeters but makes an arithmetical error which results in an incorrect answer.

Level 2: This response offers limited or inconsistent evidence of knowledge of the mathematics related to this task.

Characteristics:
The student solves for c^2 (rather than c but recognizes the congruence of diagonals and knows how to convert.

Or

The student is able to get the answer in feet but does not convert to centimeters.

Level 1: This response offers little or no evidence of knowledge of the mathematics related to this task.

Characteristics:
Student solves a right triangle correctly, but there is little evidence that the student knows how to proceed in solving the problem.

Or

There is little evidence that the student knows how to apply the Pythagorean Theorem.

SIERPINSKI TRIANGLE

MATHEMATICS STANDARDS ASSESSED

- Number and Operation Concepts
- Geometry and Measurement Concepts
- Function and Algebra Concepts
- Problem Solving and Mathematical Reasoning
- Mathematical Skills and Tools
- Mathematical Communication

DIRECTIONS TO THE STUDENT

The diagram below shows the first three stages in a pattern which leads to a fractal known as the Sierpinski triangle. Fractals are complex geometric shapes which are created by repeating some geometric process an infinite number of times.

For the Sierpinski triangle, the process being repeated to get from one stage to the next is:
For each unshaded triangle in the figure, find the midpoint of each of its sides, then connect those points to form a new triangle, and shade the interior of that triangle.

a. Sketch the next stage of this pattern.
b. If the area of the original unshaded triangle (stage 1) is 1 sq unit, what is the area of the unshaded parts of
    (1) stage 2
    (2) stage 3
    (3) stage 4
    (4) stage 5
    (5) stage 10
    (6) stage n , where n is any natural number.
c. How much of the actual Sierpinski triangle is shaded? Remember that the Sierpinski triangle results from the geometric process, defined above, being repeated an infinite number of times. Give a mathematical justification for your answer--be as specific as possible.

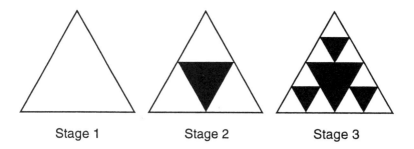

| Stage 1 | Stage 2 | Stage 3 |

MATHEMATICAL CONCEPTS

This task requires the student to discover a pattern in order to find the areas at any iteration or stage of the process which defines this fractal. The student must then consider the limit of areas in order to predict what will happen at infinity.

SOLUTION

a.

Stage 4

b. (1) $3/4 = 3/4 \times 1$
   (2) $9/16 = 3/4 \times 3/4$
   (3) $27/64 = 3/4 \times 3/4 \times 3/4$
   (4) $81/256 = (3/4)^4$
   (5) $59049 / 1,048,576 = (3/4)^{10}$
   (6) $(3/4)^n$

c. The actual Sierpinski triangle should be completely shaded since the unshaded areas are becoming very small as n increases. The limit of $(3/4)^n$ as n approaches infinity is zero and therefore, the shaded area at infinity equals the original area of one minus zero. (Note: One could also analyze the unshaded area in terms of the geometric sequence whose initial term is 1 and whose common ratio is 3/4.)

RUBRIC

Level 4: This response offers clear and convincing evidence of a deep knowledge of the mathematics related to this task.

Characteristics:
All questions are answered correctly with an appropriate mathematical justification given in part c. A minor flaw in calculation may occur.

Level 3: This response offers evidence of substantial knowledge of the mathematics related to this task.

Characteristics:
Parts a and b are correct but c is vague or weak.

Level 2: This response offers limited or inconsistent evidence of knowledge of the mathematics related to this task.

Characteristics:
Part a is correct, parts of b are incorrect or incomplete, and the answer to c is correct but the justification is weak.
Or
Part a is incorrect but all or most of b is correct based on the error in a, and the answer to c may be vague or weak.
Or
Parts a and b are correct except for a minor flaw but c is missing or indicates a serious misconception.

Level 1: This response offers little or no evidence of knowledge of the mathematics related to this task.

Characteristics:
At least 2 of the 3 parts are incorrect indication serious misconceptions, or are missing.

TAKE ME OUT TO THE BALL GAME

MATHEMATICS STANDARDS ASSESSED

- Number and Operation Concepts
- Geometry and Measurement Concepts
- Function and Algebra Concepts
- Problem Solving and Mathematical Reasoning
- Mathematical Skills and Tools
- Mathematical Communication

DIRECTIONS TO THE STUDENT

The four bases of a major league baseball field form a square which is 90 feet on each side. The pitching mound is not halfway between home plate and third base, but is 60.5 feet from home plate. Which base is the pitcher closest to? Mathematically justify your answer and provide a labeled diagram which models the problem and shows all variables to which you will refer.

MATHEMATICAL CONCEPTS

Students may analyze this problem in terms of specific distances determined by use of the Law of Cosines and its special case, the Pythagorean Theorem. Or they may analyze it in terms of angular relationships knowing that if two angles of a triangle are unequal, then the measures of the sides opposite those angles are unequal in the same order.

SOLUTIONS

The diagram should look like:

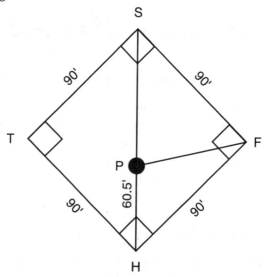

The pitcher is closest to first and third bases. Students may explain this in various ways.

One method is to compare the actual distances. Application of the law of cosines gives the distance between the pitcher's mound and first base:

$c^2 = (60.5)^2 + (90)^2 - 2(60.5)(90) \cos 45° \approx$ **63.7 ft.**

The Pythagorean Theorem gives the distance between home and second, call it d: $d^2 = 90^2 + 90^2$, which implies that d ≈127.3 ft. This distance minus 60.5, gives the distance between the pitcher's mound and second base, ≈ **66.8 ft.**

The distance to third base is also ≈ **63.7 ft** due to diagonal line symmetry.

Another method would be to compare angular size and the length of the sides opposite those angles. For example, within triangle SFP, m ∠ PSF < m ∠ SFP and so PF must be smaller than PS. m ∠ PSF < m ∠ SFP since m ∠ HPF >90° which implies that m∠ SPF < 90°. This together with the fact that m ∠ PSF = 45° implies that m ∠ SFP > 45°.

RUBRIC

Level 4: This response offers clear and convincing evidence of a deep knowledge of the mathematics related to this task.

Characteristics:
Diagram is complete and correct showing variables referred to in student's mathematical justification. A variable(s) may be missing but the student's work makes its meaning clear. In addition, student gives the correct answer and mathematically justifies it.

Level 3: This response offers evidence of substantial knowledge of the mathematics related to this task.

Characteristics:
Diagram is complete and correct showing variables referred to in student's mathematical justification. A variable(s) may be missing but the student's work makes its meaning clear. In addition, the student makes a computational error in application of the Law of Cosines or the Pythagorean Theorem, but the answer and mathematical justification are correct based on those errors.

Or

Diagram is complete and correct showing variables referred to in student's mathematical justification. A variable(s) may be missing but the student's work makes its meaning clear. In addition, student compares the pitcher's position relative to two bases only. The answer given is correct as is the mathematical justification with respect to those two bases, but the third base is not considered.

Or

Diagram is incomplete or missing but the answer is correct with appropriate justification.

Level 2: This response offers limited or inconsistent evidence of knowledge of the mathematics related to this task.

Characteristics:
Diagram is complete and correct showing variables referred to in student's mathematical justification. A variable(s) may be missing. In addition, student answers the question correctly but gives a weak mathematical justification.

Level 1: This response offers little or no evidence of knowledge of the mathematics related to this task.

Characteristics:
Student shows diagram but the remainder of the problem is not done or an answer is given without an acceptable mathematical justification.

Or

Diagram is missing, and an answer is given but without an acceptable mathematical justification.

Appendix

Student Hand-Outs

Please feel free to photocopy the material in this Appendix
and distribute to your students.

BALL BEARINGS

Ball bearings are one of the few improvements that have been made to the wheel since its invention. They may be of any size and are widely used in the construction of machines so that friction is minimized when these machines are in operation. They are so important that in World War II, the Allies bombed ball bearing manufacturing plants in Germany because they knew that destruction of these plants would paralyze truck and tank construction.

A steel ball bearing is made from a cylindrical slug of steel which is heated and formed into the shape of a ball. What is the radius of the biggest ball bearing that can be made from a cylindrical slug of radius of 2 cm and height of 2.25 cm? Show the equations that lead to your solution, round to the nearest hundredth, and indicate units throughout.

THE CHALLENGER

America experienced one of its saddest moments on January 28, 1986 when the space shuttle Challenger exploded 73 seconds after take-off. All seven crew members were killed including Christa McAuliffe, the first teacher astronaut. President Reagan appointed the Rogers Commission to investigate the disaster. They concluded that the accident resulted from an explosion caused by the combustion of gas which had leaked through a joint in one of the booster rockets. That joint was sealed by a washer-like device called an O-ring. O-ring performance was a large part of the discussion the night before the launch during a three hour conference between engineers, scientists, and public relations people involved in the operation of the space shuttle. It was decided to go ahead with the launch even though some thought that the forecasted temperature for launch time, 31°F, would make the O-rings too hard to form a leak proof seal of the joints of the booster rockets.

a. The data presented in graph A below was a large part of the discussion the night before the launch.

(1) Some thought that the data did not indicate that temperature affected O-ring performance. Why do you think they reached this conclusion? Explain.

(2) Others thought that the data indicated that the launch be postponed until the temperature was above 53°F. Why do you think they reached this conclusion? Explain.

b. The Rogers Commission was critical of the fact that the data analyzed in making the decision to launch was restricted to the data shown in graph A. The Commission felt that the data that should have been analyzed is that shown in graph B.

(1) After examining the data in graph B, explain why the Commission thought that the data in graph A was incomplete.

(2) Given the data in graph B, would you have recommended launching at 31°F ? Explain.

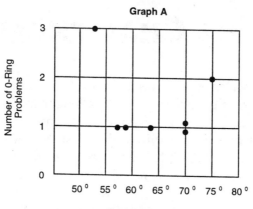

Graph A

Number of 0-Ring Problems

Temperature in ºF
at Launch Time

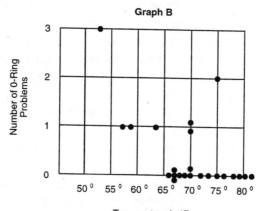

Graph B

Number of 0-Ring Problems

Temperature in ºF
at Launch Time

Coin Toss

Suppose that a fair coin is flipped.

a. If the coin is flipped 3 times, what is the probability that
   (1) at least two of the flips are heads.
   (2) At least two of the flips are heads given that one of the flips is a head.

b. If the coin were flipped 25 times, what is the probability that all 25 flips would result in heads? Explain your answer.

c. A game is won if each time a fair coin is flipped it comes up heads. Find the minimum number of flips required for the probability of winning the game to be less than .002.

COLUMBUS SAILED THE OCEAN BLUE

The first landfall of Christopher Columbus on the shore of a Bahamian island on Friday, October 12, 1492, has had an immense impact on world history. His first voyage to this continent took slightly over 33 days. Columbus sailed a southwestward course from the island of Gomera in the Canaries to an island in the Bahamas. Many historians think that the island upon which Columbus made landfall is Samana Cay. In recent years, the trip from Gomera to Samana Cay has taken modern sailing ships and racing yachts about the same time it took Columbus! Columbus' ships averaged about 3 1/2 knots during the 33 day crossing. (A knot is a speed of 1 nautical mile per hour. A nautical mile is equal to 1,852 meters or about 6,076 feet, and a statute (land) mile is 5,280 feet.)

a. In statute miles, about how far is it from Gomera to Samana Cay? Indicating units of measure throughout, show how you arrived at your answer. Round your answer to the nearest hundred statute miles.

b. If you traveled this distance southwest of your home, where would you be? Show the route on a map and indicate, on the map, the proportion you used to scale the distance.

THE ENDANGERED FRACTION

Throughout the history of American stock exchanges, stock prices have been quoted in multiples of 1/8 of a dollar or 12.5 cents. This tradition dates back to pre-Revolutionary days when dollar coins could be physically cut into "pieces of eight" to make change. However, foreign stock exchanges price their stock in decimal amounts with pennies being the smallest units in which they trade. American stock exchanges are increasingly under pressure to join foreign markets in decimal pricing.

Answer the following questions, showing the procedures that lead to your answers.

1. Suppose that you bought 10,000 shares of a stock when it was selling at its yearly low of 41 1/2, and that it is now worth 85 7/8.
      a. In dollars and cents, how much did you profit by this increase?
      b. By what percent did your investment increase? (Round to the nearest percent.)
2. Could a stock listed on an American stock exchange sell for $20.78? Explain.
3. Some American exchanges are now allowing for prices to be quoted in multiples of 1/16 of a point. Could a stock listed on such an exchange sell for $20.78? Explain.
4. Name 5 amounts that can be expressed in dollars and a whole number of cents that can be used in exchanges that allow for pricing in multiples of 1/8.
5. Write a rule for every dollar and whole cent amount that represents a selling price on a market which prices in multiples of one eighth? (You may state the rule as an equation or you may express it in words.)
6. Representatives in Congress as well as many financial

experts believe that American investors would be better served if our pricing of stock were done as it is in foreign stock markets. Why do you think this is the case? (Keep in mind that the price at which investors can buy stock is more than the price at which they can sell that particular stock to a broker and that difference is calculated in eighths.)

THE EYES HAVE IT

Each person inherits **two** genes, one from each parent, which determine their eye color. Each gene is either dominant, type B for brown, or recessive, type b for blue. There are two ways that a person can have brown eyes: they may either be *brown eyed dominant* which means they have two brown genes *(BB)*, or *brown eyed recessive* which means that one gene is brown and one gene is blue *(Bb)*. But there is only one way that a person can have blue eyes: both of the genes they inherit from their parents must be blue *(bb)*. The gene that a child inherits from a parent is a random choice of one of the parent's two genes.

Show your process in finding the probability that a child has

(a) blue eyes if her mother is *brown eyed recessive (Bb)*, and her father is blue eyed.

(b) blue eyes if her paternal grandmother is *brown eyed recessive (Bb)*, her paternal grandfather is blue eyed, her maternal grandmother is *brown eyed dominant (BB)*, and her maternal grandfather is *brown eyed recessive(Bb)*.

THE FERRIS WHEEL

The Ferris Wheel, a classic amusement park ride, was invented by George Ferris. Mr. Ferris was an American engineer who debuted his wheel at the 1893 World's Fair in Chicago.

Suppose that you are 4 feet off the ground in the bottom car of a Ferris Wheel and ready to ride. If the radius of the wheel is 25 ft and it makes 2 revolutions per minute,

a. Sketch a graph that shows your height h (in ft) above the ground at time t (in sec) during the first 45 seconds of your ride.
b. Why is your curve periodic? Explain in terms of the problem.
c. What is the period of your curve? Explain this number in terms of the problem.
d. Give a possible equation for your curve.
e.   At what speed are you traveling on the Ferris Wheel? (ft/sec) Explain.
f.   Suppose that the radius of the Wheel were decreased and that the Wheel still makes two revolutions per minute, would the

(1) period change? Explain. (If yes, indicate if it would increase or decrease.)

(2) amplitude change? Explain. (If yes, indicate if it would increase or decrease.)

(3) speed change? Explain. (If yes, indicate if it would increase or decrease.)

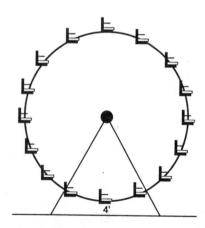

A FIELD TRIP

A bus company has contracted with a local high school to carry 450 students on a field trip. The company has 18 large busses which can carry up to 30 students and 19 small busses which can carry up to 15 students. There are only 20 drivers available on the day of the field trip.

A) If x large busses and y small busses are used, write a system of inequalities that models all of the information given above.

B) Shade the set of points in the plane that contains all possible solutions to the inequalities asked for in part A.

C) The total cost of operating the large busses is $225 a day, and the total cost of operating the small busses is $100 per day.

(1) Explain how to use this additional information in conjunction with the graph, asked for in part B, to determine how many busses of each type should be used to minimize the cost of transporting all 450 students. Label all points on your graph that are important to the solution of the problem.

(2) Determine the minimum cost of transporting all 450 students. Be sure that your work is complete and clear.

GET A JOB

Suppose you are driving on the New Jersey Turnpike to go to a new job interview in New York at 11:30 a.m. You know that you can average 55 mph on the turnpike. You must drive 50 miles to the exit you must use; it will take about 25 minutes of driving to get to the location of your appointment after you leave the turnpike. You also know that the gas tank holds 20 gallons and that you get about 18 miles per gallon on the highway.

Based on this information and the information in the picture below, do you need to stop and buy gasoline on the way to New York? If you do stop to buy gasoline, remember it will take some time to do so. Will you make it to your appointment early, on time, or late? If early or late, about how early or late would you expect to be? Explain your answers carefully.

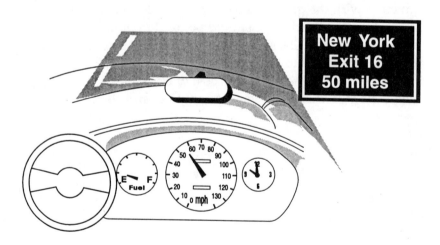

IN YOUR BEST INTEREST

You have earned $1,500 and want the money to grow by depositing it into a savings account at one of two banks. The *Invest With Us* bank offers an interest rate of 5.5% compounded annually. The *Make Your Money Grow* bank offers an interest rate of 5.4%. How often must the *Make Your Money Grow* bank compound your interest in order for you to make more money by investing with them? Include all possible answers, indicate your process, and explain your answer. (Please work with dollars and cents, and remember that banks round fractions of a cent down to the next penny when determining your interest.)

LET'S GET PHYSICAL

The results of a questionnaire filled out by a student body of one thousand students determined that their most frequent methods of exercise were running, lifting, and skating. The results showed that

260 students ran.
360 students lifted.
240 students skated.
100 students ran and lifted.
 80 students ran and skated.
120 students lifted and skated.
 60 students ran, lifted, and skated.

1. Construct a Venn Diagram and record the number of students in each region.

2. a. How many students only lift to exercise?
    b. How many students run or lift to exercise?
    c. How many students run and lift, but do not skate to exercise?
    d. How many students do not run, lift, or skate?

3. If you were in charge of scheduling exercise availability and could only schedule 2 activities for any time slot, which two of the three most popular exercises would you schedule most frequently? Explain and justify your answer.

MATRICES IN
MANUFACTURING

A computer manufacturer has three factories at which their products are made. Number of units sold last year (in thousands) are stated in the matrix below.

	Factory A	Factory B	Factory C	
Laptop	5	4	6	
Desk Top	10	12	11	= N
Printer	8	10	10	
Scanner	3	2.5	2.1	

a. The selling price of a laptop is $2200, a desk top is $2600, a printer is $450, and a scanner is $730. Show this information in a matrix P.

b. Use matrices N and P to find matrix R which gives the total revenue (in thousands) at each factory. Be sure that your process is evident, that each matrix is written out, and that R is identified.

c. With respect to matrix R and this problem, what information is given by the value a_{12}?

d. In dollars, what was this company's total revenue last year?

MEAN SALARIES

The annual salaries of all the employees of a small company are listed below.

President: $110,000
Vice President: $60,000
Senior Professionals $50,000; $48,000; $48,000; $44,000
Junior Professionals: $36,000; $36,000; $36,000; $32,000
Clerical Staff: $22,000; $18,000; $14,000

a. What are the mean, the median, and the mode of the salaries of the employees of this company?
b. How is each of these statistics affected if the President's salary is excluded?
c. What do your findings tell you about the statistic that should probably be used in discussions of the salary of a typical professional baseball player? Explain.

A PAINTER'S SOLUTION

Raphael visited the White House and was awed by the beauty of the Blue Room. He was so awed, that he is going to paint his living room the very same shade of blue. Since he is a very busy person, he plans to spread the work out so that he can do some painting each day until the job is done. He will start with the largest wall and paint half of it today. Tomorrow, he will paint half of what remains to be painted on that wall. And he will continue in this fashion, each day painting half of the unpainted part of the wall, until he completely paints the wall. When can he start painting the next wall? Provide a diagram and a mathematical justification for your answer.

PENNY WISE

The Sears Tower in Chicago, Illinois is the tallest building in the United States. It was built in 1974 and measures 1,454 feet in height from sidewalk to roof. Suppose that a penny is to be dropped off the roof of the tower. Assume negligible air resistance, show how you arrived at your answer indicating the units throughout, and round to the nearest tenth when you answer the following questions.

a. How high is the penny 3 seconds after it is dropped?
b. How long does it take the penny to hit the sidewalk?
c. What is the velocity of the penny when it hits the sidewalk?
d. What is the speed of the penny, in miles per hour, when it hits the sidewalk?
e. What do you think happens when the penny hits the sidewalk?

POOL CONSTRUCTION

Suppose that a community is thinking of hiring your company to increase the size of their swimming pool. The dimensions of the existing pool are given below. The community has undergone considerable growth and they would like to increase pool memberships by 25%. In addition, they want to maintain the current hours of operation and make the pool available to all members during those times. Write a proposal for presentation to the mayor and council. Be sure that your proposal:

    a. includes a labeled diagram,

    b. explains why the new pool will accommodate 25% more members,

    c. gives the surface area of the new pool as compared to that of the present pool,

    d. gives the amount of water needed to fill the new pool as compared to that needed to fill the existing pool, and

    e. indicates all units of measure.

The surface area of the water in the pool is a 24′ by 48′ rectangle. The side view of the pool is uniform and shows its dimensions.

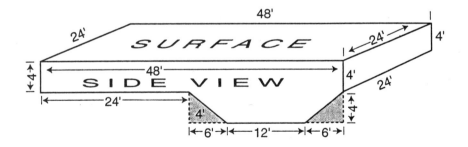

PRICE RESTORATION

For a sale, a shopkeeper lowered the original price of an item by 30 percent. After the sale, the shop keeper told his clerk, Mike, to raise the price of that item by 30 percent of its sale price. So, Mike marked the item with its original price. Was Mike right or wrong in doing that? Present a convincing argument to support your answer; you may wish to include a simple, specific example as part of your argument.

A RECTANGULAR PLOT

Suppose that you want to enclose a 650 sq m rectangular plot of land along a river. What can the dimensions of the plot be if you have only 110 m of fencing and you do not fence the river side? Provide a labeled diagram and show the method you used to arrive at your answer. If a graphing utility is used, indicate how it was used, and if applicable, sketch and label curves and any significant points. (Round answers to the nearest tenth.)

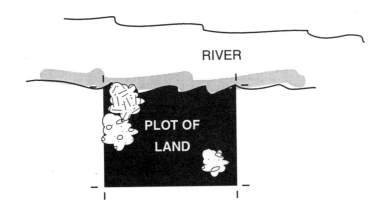

SEE THE LIGHT

An artisan has been hired to repair a leaded glass window which looks as pictured below. The glass is held in the window by its wooden frame and by six diagonal lead strips. If the artisan must replace all six diagonal strips and the lead is sold in centimeter lengths only, what is the total length of lead she must provide? Round your final answer to the nearest whole centimeter which will allow for enough lead to complete the job and indicate the processes you used to get your answer.

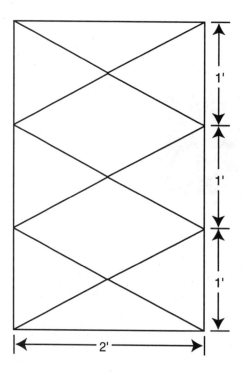

SIERPINSKI TRIANGLE

The diagram below shows the first three stages in a pattern which leads to a fractal known as the Sierpinski triangle. Fractals are complex geometric shapes which are created by repeating some geometric process an infinite number of times.

For the Sierpinski triangle, the process being repeated to get from one stage to the next is:
For each unshaded triangle in the figure, find the midpoint of each of its sides, then connect those points to form a new triangle, and shade the interior of that triangle.

a. Sketch the next stage of this pattern.
b. If the area of the original unshaded triangle (stage 1) is 1 sq unit, what is the area of the unshaded parts of
    (1) stage 2
    (2) stage 3
    (3) stage 4
    (4) stage 5
    (5) stage 10
    (6) stage n , where n is any natural number.
c.   How much of the actual Sierpinski triangle is shaded? Remember that the Sierpinski triangle results from the geometric process, defined above, being repeated an infinite number of times. Give a mathematical justification for your answer--be as specific as possible.

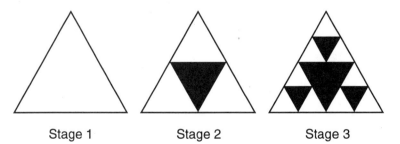

Stage 1   Stage 2   Stage 3

TAKE ME OUT TO THE BALL GAME

The four bases of a major league baseball field form a square which is 90 feet on each side. The pitching mound is not halfway between home plate and third base, but is 60.5 feet from home plate. Which base is the pitcher closest to? Mathematically justify your answer and provide a labeled diagram which models the problem and shows all variables to which you will refer.